Ira Maurice Price

A Syllabus of Old Testament History

Outlines and Literature, with an Introductory Treatment of Biblical Geography

Ira Maurice Price

A Syllabus of Old Testament History
Outlines and Literature, with an Introductory Treatment of Biblical Geography

ISBN/EAN: 9783337204655

Printed in Europe, USA, Canada, Australia, Japan

Cover: Foto ©ninafisch / pixelio.de

More available books at **www.hansebooks.com**

A SYLLABUS

OF

OLD TESTAMENT HISTORY:

OUTLINES AND LITERATURE,

WITH AN

Introductory Treatment of Biblical Geography,

BY

IRA M. PRICE, PH.D., *LEIPSIC*,

PROFESSOR OF HEBREW AND THE COGNATE LANGUAGES IN THE THEOLOGICAL
SEMINARY, MORGAN PARK, CHICAGO.

Give diligence to present thyself approved unto God, a workman that needeth not to be ashamed, handling aright the word of truth.—2 TIM. ii. 15.

:: **Fleming H. Revell** ::

NEW YORK:	CHICAGO:
12 BIBLE HOUSE, ASTOR PLACE.	148 AND 150 MADISON STREET.

= **Publisher of Evangelical Literature** =

Entered according to Act of Congress, in the year 1890, by
FLEMING H. REVELL,
In the office of the Librarian of Congress, at Washington, D. C.

To the Classes
in Old Testament History,

WHICH HAVE PURSUED, DURING THE PAST FOUR YEARS,
WITH SO MUCH INTEREST AND ENTHUSIASM,
THE STUDY OF THE HISTORICAL
PORTION OF

The Old Revelation,

UNDER THE DIRECTION OF
THE AUTHOR.

PREFACE.

We have reached a new era in Bible study. Old plans and methods of work are giving place to the new. The old material of the Bible has become enriched by the wealth of antiquity. The nations of the Orient are rising from their slumbers. The voices of peoples, old when the first word of the Old Testament was penned, are heard in the East. Their testimony is essential to any correct estimate of those times. In fact, the field of study has so enlarged and expanded that the old text-book method of studying Old Testament History must be superseded by one more stimulating and comprehensive. The student should be turned loose in the luxuriant fields of modern investigation and discovery. He should produce his picture of Old Testament History filled with all the events of contemporaneous peoples. This Syllabus aims to furnish a practical compendium and plan of work to accomplish just this end. It is designed as a new textbook for use in Seminaries, Colleges, Academies and Training Schools. The Bible narrative alone can be studied, or in addition thereto any prescribed amount of outside reading done. The option of teacher or student can be followed.

The plan of work is very simple. Before one attempts to study the Old Testament he should have some definite knowledge of the lands of the Bible. The barest external facts respecting the chief book to be studied should be made familiar. And the section of history to be analyzed and synchronized must be divided into periods possessing characteristics all their own. Hence the INTRODUCTION takes up and studies Biblical Geography, gives some of the simplest chronological facts about the Old Testament, and divides the history to be treated into twelve periods, or epochs, each possessing peculiarities its own.

The body of the book presents these periods divided into sections, the sections into paragraphs, the paragraphs into sub-heads, etc. This analysis does not claim perfection. Its degree of detail is not everywhere uniform. The demands of the narrative are not everywhere the same, so that no one method has been pursued to monotony. The whole aims to be an orderly and convenient arrangement and classification of the most important facts in Old Testament History. It will serve as a basis, or starting-point, for supplemental reading on the part of the student.

Questions of criticism and chronology are, for the most, purposely omitted. At this stage of the study they would prove to be only a source of confusion. The *literature* referred to is generally that which should be most accessible to the ordinary student. Josephus' Antiquities, however, should be read alongside the corresponding Bible account. All this cited literature is barely an introduction to the vast field now open to the student of Old Testament History.

These outlines are not expository in the ordinary sense of that term. They are intended to lead the student along the line of the facts. He familiarizes himself with the Old Testament narrative, and with all the new light shed on its pages by contemporaneous history and modern discovery and research. This is just the point at which most Bible students are deficient. Moralize and allegorize they can, easily. But to give and explain the Bible facts accurately, and in order, is a rare ability. Some of the prevalent erroneous and disastrous allegorizing methods of our day will meet their doom when their advocates and employers become grounded in a knowledge of the historical setting of the Old Testament. As soon as the careful and devoted student has mastered the events and the facts, the impulses and the motives and the moral at the bottom of these facts readily appear, the lessons and teachings, thus concretely expressed, present themselves with a vividness and force never before conceived.

The APPENDIX presents, in an abbreviated, concise and convenient form, the synchronism of Judah and Israel. The LIST OF WORKS gathers up the authorities referred to throughout the Syllabus, and adds a SUPPLEMENTAL LIST of some of the more elaborate, the more scholarly, and the latest works of value for more extensive and detailed study of Old Testament History. The GENERAL INDEX includes the historical names and topics mentioned only in the Syllabus. For the preparation of the INDEX OF SCRIPTURE TEXTS, and for the verification of the Bible references, the thanks of the author are due Mr. L. C. Randolph of the Seminary. Other obligations are sufficiently recognized by references.

By a discriminating and careful use of the *interleaves* in jotting down new facts, explanations and references, each one can make for himself of this Syllabus a handy and indispensable compend of Old Testament History.

A similar treatment of Old Testament Prophecy is in course of preparation.

It is the purpose of the author to provide a simple, concise, practical and comprehensive method of studying the history found in the Old Testament and among contemporaneous peoples. He, therefore, invites suggestions, criticism and corrections leading to that end. More conscious than any one else of its defects, yet convinced by four years of class-room experience of its practicalness, the author now gives to the Bible studying public this little Syllabus. It is accompanied with the prayer that it may be the means of arousing a more genuine interest in the fundamental historical study of the Old Testament revelation.

THEOLOGICAL SEMINARY,   IRA M. PRICE.
   Morgan Park, Chicago, December 6, 1890.

TABLE OF CONTENTS.

INTRODUCTION.

	Pages
I. Why study Old Testament History?	5-8
II. Biblical Geography	8-20

Secs.
1. The Old Testament World 10-11
2. Geography of Palestine 11-13
3. Geography of Palestine—continued 13-15
4. Natural History of Palestine 15-16
5. Climate of Palestine 16
6. The Political Divisions of Palestine 17-18
7. The Chief Points and Cities of Palestine 18-19
8. Jerusalem 19-20

    III. Literature 21-23

9. The Books of the Bible 21
10. The Books and Chapters in the Old Testament .. 21-22
11. Moderate General Outfit for the Study of Old Testament History 23

    IV. Chronological 24-25

12. Period of Time covered by the Bible 24
13. Periods of Old Testament History 24-25

FIRST PERIOD, ANTE-DILUVIAN.

14. The Creation 27-28
15. Eden 29-30
16. The Temptation and the Fall 30-31
17. Cain and his Descendants 31-32
18. Seth and his Descendants 33

SECOND PERIOD, POST-DILUVIAN.

19. The Deluge 34-35
20. The Second Beginning 35-36
21. The Table of Nations 36-38
22. The Tower of Babel and the Dispersion 38-39

THIRD PERIOD, PATRIARCHAL.

23. Abraham's Call and Wanderings	40-41
24. Abraham's settled Life in Canaan	41-43
25. Career of Isaac	43-45
26. The Wanderings of Jacob to the History of Joseph	45-46
27. Jacob and Joseph to the Descent into Egypt	46-47

FOURTH PERIOD, BONDAGE.

28. Descent and Settlement in Egypt	48-49
29. The Sojourn in Egypt	49-50

FIFTH PERIOD, WANDERINGS.

30. The Exodus	51-53
31. The March to Sinai	53-54
32. Doings at Sinai in the Book of Exodus	54-56
33. Doings and Laws given at Sinai in Lev. and Num. i-ix.	56-57
34. From Sinai to the Arnon	57-59
35. Conquests East of the Jordan	59-61
36. Final Review and Death of Moses	61-62

SIXTH PERIOD, CONQUEST.

37. The Entrance into Canaan	63-64
38. The Southern Campaign	64-66
39. The Northern Campaign	66-67
40. Settlement of the Tribes	67-69
41. Joshua's Departure and Condition of the Land	69-70
42. Supplementary to the Conquest	70-71

SEVENTH PERIOD, JUDGES.

43. First three Oppressions and three Judges	72-73
44. Canaanite and Midianite Oppressions	73-75
45. Ammonite and Philistine Oppressions	75-77
46. Ruth	77-78
47. Eli and the Fall of Shiloh	78-80
48. Samuel as Judge and Ruler to the Accession of Saul	80-81
49. Samuel under a King, Saul	81-83

EIGHTH PERIOD, KINGDOM.

50. Saul's sane Career	84-86

51. Saul's insane Career	86-88
52. David's pre-regal Career	88-90
53. David's prosperous Reign	90-93
54. David's calamitous Reign	93-96
55. The Reign of Solomon	96-99
56. Solomon's Temple	99-102

NINTH PERIOD, DUAL KINGDOM.

57. Dual religious Decline	103-105
58. { Reign of Asa in Judah, / Destruction of three Dynasties in Israel, }	106-108
59. Reign of the House of Omri of Israel	108-112
60. Reign of Jehoshaphat of Judah	112-114
61. The great Period of oral Prophets and oral Prophecy	114-119
62. { Religious Decline in Judah, / Check to Idolatry in Israel, }	119-122
63. Religious Decline and regal Prosperity	122-125
64. { Anarchy in Israel, / Idolatry in Judah, }	126-128

TENTH PERIOD, JUDAH ALONE.

65. { Reforms in Judah. / Downfall of Israel, }	129-132
66. Hezekiah's Reign after the Fall of Samaria	132-135
67. Reigns of Manasseh and Amon	135-137
68. Josiah's Reign and Reform	137-140
69. Decline under Jehoahaz and Jehoiakim	140-141
70. Decline under Jehoiachin and Zedekiah	142-144

ELEVENTH PERIOD, THE EXILE.

71. Fall of Jerusalem	145-147
72. Remnants in Palestine and Egypt	147-149
73. Babylonian Exile of the Jews	149-151

TWELFTH PERIOD, RETURN.

74. Fall of Babylon	152-153
75. The first Return	153-154
76. Building of the second Temple	155-156
77. Queen Esther	156-157

78. Second Return—under Ezra........................ 157-158
79. Third Return—Nehemiah........................... 158-160
80. General Review................................... 160-161

APPENDIX.
The Chronology of Judah and Israel.

Section I. Dual Kingdom............................. 162-165
" II. Judah alone 166-167
" III. Exile..... 167-168
" IV. Restoration.............................. 169
" V. Kings of Judah........................... 170
" VI. Dynasties of Israel..... 171

INDEXES.

List of Works referred to............................ 172-176
Supplemental List.................................... 177-180
Index of Names and Topics............................ 181-188
Index of Scripture Texts............................. 189-198

INTRODUCTION.

I. WHY STUDY OLD TESTAMENT HISTORY?

The doings and sayings of individuals and peoples constitute the basis of history. They are the elements which give character to any time or period. We must know the men, and the times, and the customs of any people before our judgment on the character of any period of that people's history can be of real value. Their literature and religion are vitally connected with their daily life and activity; in fact, they grow out of the real life of the people. If we would understand their literature and religion, we must make a close study of their habits and customs, in other words, of their history.

This is as true of Old Testament as of secular history. The first and important work of every Bible student is to study the times and customs of the Bible, to bring up vividly before him the individual events of that history. For the doing of this work there are several important reasons:

a. We have here the oldest history of mankind. It contains an epitome of the world's history from the beginning down to the call of Abraham, and a condensed history of Abraham's descendants down to the close of the fourth century before Christ. It is brief, but exceedingly comprehensive. It sweeps through centuries of important and epitomized events.

b. It is the most complete history of the oriental world in our possession. It is not confined to one people, but is full of references to many and great peoples. In fact, it is the only trustworthy source of information regarding several of those almost prehistoric nations. It is the beaten track through oriental times, to which and from which numerous pathways lead. Taking it as starting-point, and making it our own, we shall have little difficulty in increasing our knowledge of the contemporaneous history of the surrounding peoples.

c. It is the history of God's chosen people. Gen. i-xi. 9, is the biblical introduction to the history of Israel. With the call of Abraham the chosen people are set apart. From this point to the end of the Old Testament we are following Israel. They are the peculiar objects of care. Around them Jehovah makes everything revolve. Other peoples are mentioned only in so far as they come in contact with, or are related to, the house of Jacob. The history of Israel is full of instruction, admonition, encouragement, warning, promise and benediction to every one who will make of it a careful study.

d. It is the soil out of which grew the prophetic and poetical writings of the Old Testament. It furnishes us the conditions of this growth and gives us the principles by which it was made. The prophetic utterances of the Old Testament are not isolated, but are vitally connected with some period and time.

e. It is essential to any true method of interpreting the Old Testament. No one can understand the import, the full significance, of the words of the prophets without a reasonably complete knowledge of the times which called out their utterances. Their prophecies and predictions *cannot be understood* without a comprehension of the times in which they grew up. The ignorance current regarding Old Testament History has been the most fruitful source of bad and false interpretations in this portion of Scripture. Out of isolated and disconnected passages, regardless of the historic background, men have woven theories, spiritualized and allegorized until, in many minds, the Old Testament is a mere jumble of uncertain sounds. On the other hand, the history gives us the events and the customs of the people which provoked the words of the prophet; it gives us the basis for his utterances, and the only true data by which we can rightly interpret his words. Old Testament History is the basis and background of a correct interpretation of the Old Testament.

f. It will be the means of strengthening our faith in the Bible. In former times the charge of fable, fancy and fiction was made against this old revelation, as a whole. But no informed man, who is sane, will make this statement to-day. The old Bible has witnesses to its truth coming forth from almost every ancient oriental land. Its statements are confirmed and re-affirmed by the discoveries in every portion of the Old Testament world. Its history is supplemented and complemented and corroborated until, with renewed strength and faith, we can affirm and maintain its truth in the presence of every honest searcher after truth.

g. It is the first part of our great revelation, the introduction to the coming of our Lord. It is a vital part of God's revealed word. The Bible is *one* book. It must be studied *as one book*. The Old Testament preceded the New, and prepared the way for it. It supplies material, types, illustrations and predictions for the New Testament. It is essential to an understanding of the New Testament. In fact, without it the New Testament cannot be correctly interpreted.

II. BIBLICAL GEOGRAPHY.

History is local. Historical events, to be well understood, must be localized. Events are dependent for many of their characteristics upon the topography of the places in which they occurred. The reader or student of history must associate the event with its geographical surroundings. This is the only sure method of fixing and firmly grasping a series of occurrences. The mind of man makes pictures — puts things into groups. And these groups always have a background against which they should be seen. The background is the mountain, the plain or the plateau.

Bible history has been too long suspended in midair. Much of the current ignorance of its facts has been due to a neglect of the study of the geography of Palestine and adjacent lands. In other words, the background of the picture was lacking; there was no local coloring. Readers and students rambled through a mass of chaotic facts, and brought out with them only a very general impression of all that they had seen. By a systematic and orderly study of the background, at the start, we shall be prepared to locate our events as they occur, and pin them to their proper places.

An important essential to a proper understanding of Old Testament History is a knowledge of the lands of the Bible. These are Palestine, and all the lands which are prominently mentioned in connection with the nations of the Old Testament. It has been found to be the most profitable introduction to the study of the history in the Old Testament.

Hence at this point this topic will be taken up and followed out with as much thoroughness of treatment as time and space will allow. Cf. Stanley, Sinai and Palestine, Preface.

§1. THE OLD TESTAMENT WORLD.

1. *Extent:* *a.* by parallels; *b.* by miles; *c.* by sq. miles.
2. *Chief bodies of water* — seven: *a.* location; *b.* size; *c.* characteristics.
3. *Principal mountain ranges* — six: *a.* location; *b.* extent and height; *c.* characteristics.
4. *Main rivers* — six: *a.* source, direction and outlet; *b.* length and use.
5. *Mountain countries* — three : *a.* names and boundaries; *b.* contour and characteristics; *c.* principal cities.
6. *Plain countries* — five: *a.* names and boundaries; *b.* contour and characteristics; *c.* principal cities.
7. *Mediterranean coast lands* — six: *a.* names and boundaries; *b.* contour and characteristics; *c.* principal cities.

Suggestions:

1. Draw a map of the Old Testament world.

2. Make constant use of the map until the points become fixed in mind.

3. Locate from memory (1) the bodies of water,

i

(2) mountain ranges, (3) rivers, and (4) the countries in each of these divisions.

4. Give the location of the ancient capital or principal city in each of the countries.

5. Thoroughly master this section before proceeding to the next.

Literature:

Hurlbut, Manual of Biblical Geography, pp. 17–22.

Johnson, Biblical Wall Atlas. F. H. Revell, Chicago and N. Y., 1889.

Wilson, John, The Lands of the Bible, 2 vols. Edinburgh, 1847.

Kennedy, J. F., Countries and Places Mentioned in Bible History. Am. S. S. Union.

Bible Atlas, by George Grove. London, 1868.

Coleman, Lyman, An Historical Text Book and Atlas of Biblical Geography. Philadelphia, 1877.

Bible Atlas and Gazetteer, Am. Tract Society.

New Bible Atlas, *new edition*, Religious Tract Soc. London, 1890.

§2. GEOGRAPHY OF PALESTINE.

1. *Boundaries of Palestine proper.*
2. *Extent:* a. by parallels; b. by miles; c. area, (1) west of Jordan, (2) east of Jordan, (3) total; d. land of promise.

3. *Origin and significance of its names:* a. Canaan; b. Palestine; c. Holy Land.
4. *Natural divisions of Palestine — four parallels from North to South:* a. plain by the Mediterranean Sea; b. mountain range; c. Jordan valley; d. eastern table-land.
5. *Size, divisions and characteristics of the maritime plain:* a. Phœnicia; b. Esdraelon; c. Sharon; d. Philistia.
6. *Describe the mountain range, especially:* a. lower Lebanon; b. hills of lower Galilee; c. hill country of Judea and Samaria; d. low hills; e. South country.
7. *Characteristics of the Jordan valley:* a. its remarkable depression; b. its sudden fall; c. size and surroundings.
8. *Eastern table-land:* a. boundaries; b. contour; c. contents.

Literature:

Hurlbut, Manual of Bib. Geog., pp. 28–32.
Osborn, Map of Palestine.
Conder, C. R., Map of Palestine, in 26 sheets. London, 1880.
Conder, C. R., Palestine. N.Y. 1890.
Kiepert, H., Neue Wandkarte von Palaestina. Berlin, 1854.
Van de Velde, C. W. M., Map of the Holy Land, 8 sheets, second edition. London, 1865.
Robinson, Physical Geog. of Palestine. Boston, 1865.

1

Thomson, The Land and The Book, 3 vols., (new edition), N. Y. 1886.
Stanley, Sinai and Palestine, chap. i–xi. N. Y.
Robinson, Biblical Researches in Palestine, 3 vols. Boston, 1857.
Macduff, Sunsets on Hebrew Mountains.
Wilson, Jno., Lands of the Bible. 2 vols.
Merrill, East of the Jordan. N. Y., 1883.
Schumacher, Across the Jordan. London, 1886.
Tristram, The Land of Israel. London, 1886.
" Land of Moab. N. Y., 1873.
Dixon, Hepworth. The Holy Land. London, 1868.
Osborn, Guide to Palestine. Philadelphia, 1868.
Baedeker, Syria and the Holy Land. Leipzig, 1885.
Articles on "Palestine" in Encycs. and Dictionaries.

§3. GEOGRAPHY OF PALESTINE—*Continued.*

1. *Principal mountain peaks west of the Jordan*—give ten: *a.* names; *b.* height; *c.* relative location.
2. *Principal points east of the Jordan* — three: *a.* names; *b.* heights; *c.* relative position.
3. *Plains of Palestine:* *a.* Esdraelon; *b.* Sharon; *c.* Philistia; *d.* Jericho or Jordan; *e.* South country; *f.* Bashan.
4. *River of Palestine*—Jordan: *a.* sources; *b.* fall between various points; *c.* length, width and

depth; *d.* entire fall; *e.* velocity; *f.* average per mile.

5. *Brooks and wadies of Palestine:* (1) east of Jordan — three; (2) west of Jordan and emptying into it — three; (3) flowing into the Mediterranean Sea — three; *a.* names; *b.* size, length; *c.* territory drained; *d.* perpetual or perennial.

6. *Lakes of Palestine* — two: *a.* Merom (cf. Josh. xi. 5, 7); *b.* Chinnereth or Galilee (cf. Num. xxxiv. 11; Deut. iii. 17; Josh. xii. 3; xiii. 27); *a.* size; *b.* level; *c.* connection; *d.* use.

7. *The sea of Palestine* — (*Salt*, Gen. xiv. 3; of *Arabah*, Deut. iii. 17; *Eastern*, Ezek. xlvii. 18; Joel ii. 20,): *a.* size; *b.* depth; *c.* level; *d.* character of water; *e.* source of supply; *f.* outlet; *g.* its enclosure.

8. *Characteristics of Palestine:* *a.* seclusion from the rest of the world; *b.* smallness and narrowness of territory; *c.* central position, cf. 1 Kings x. 29; 2 Kings xxiii. 29.

Literature:

Additional to that given under §6.

Ritter, Geography of Palestine, vol. ii. pp. 226-336.

Lynch, Expedition to the Jordan and Dead Sea Philadelphia, 1849.

Stanley, Sinai and Palestine, chaps. vi. ix. xi.

MacGregor, J., The Rob Roy on the Jordan, Nile and Red Sea. New York, 1870.

Manning, Sam'l, Those Holy Fields.
Gage, W. L., Studies in Bible Lands. Am. Tract Society.

§4. NATURAL HISTORY OF PALESTINE.

1. *Geological features:* (1) *a.* sea coast; *b.* plains; *c.* mountain west of Jordan; *d.* mountain east of Jordan; *e.* Gilead; *f.* Hauran, Bashan; *g.* east of Dead Sea; (2) *a.* springs and fountains; *b.* sepulchres; *c.* caves; *d.* extinct volcanic remains.
2. *Botanical features:* (1) *a.* plains; *b.* hill country west; *c.* hill country east; *d.* Bashan; *e.* Jordan valley; *f.* South country; (2) *a.* chief fruits; *b.* chief flowers; *c.* chief vegetables; *d.* chief grains.
3. *Zoological features:* (1) *a.* mammalia; *b.* birds; *c.* reptiles; *d.* fishes; (2) *a.* chief domestic animals; *b.* chief wild animals; *c.* chief venomous reptiles.

Literature:

Stanley, Sinai and Palestine. Map opp. p. 178.
Hurlbut, Man. Bib. Geog. Map p. 28.
Lynch. See §6.
Tristram, Natural Hist. of the Bible. New York, 1867.
Harris,   "   "   "   "   Boston, 1820.
Groser, Trees and Plants of the Bible, in By-paths of Bible Knowledge. Religious Tract Society, London.

Tristram, Fauna and Flora of Palestine. London, 1888.
Osborn, Plants of the Bible. Philadelphia, 1865.
Barrows, Sacred Geography and Antiquities.
Hart H. C., Animals of the Bible. Rel. Tract Soc.
Wood, J..G., Bible Animals. New York, 1872.

§5. CLIMATE OF PALESTINE.

1. *Seasons:* a. Winter, Nov.–April, wet; b. summer, May—Oct., rainy and dry.
2. *Temperature:* a. average in winter 49.1°; b. greatest cold 28°; c. average July and Aug. 78.4°; d. greatest heat 92°; e. extreme range in year 52°; f. mean annual 65. 6°; g. isothermal lines in U. S. A., across Florida and Southern California; h. at different times of the day; i. at various elevations.
3. *Rain:* a. time of greatest fall; b. time of least fall; c. mean annual fall; d. direction of approach.
4. *Winds:* a. westerly in rainy seasons; b. easterly in winter; c. N. W. and S. in summer; d. sirocco.
5. *Purity of the atmosphere.*

Literature:

Robinson's Physical Geog. of Palestine.
Gage, W. L. Studies in the Holy Land.
Under art. "Palestine" in Smith's Bib. Dictionary.
Any work on the Geography of Palestine.

§6. THE POLITICAL DIVISIONS OF PALESTINE.

1. *Patriarchal period* — down to descent into Egypt: *a.* low-lands — Canaanites, Phœnicians; *b.* highlands west — Amorites, Hivites, Jebusites, Hittites; *c.* highlands east — Moabites, Amorites, Ammonites.
2. *Tribal period* — settlement of the tribes:
    (1) Tribes east of Jordan — two and one-half.
    (2) Tribes west of Jordan and south of half tribe of Manasseh — 5.
    (3) Tribes west of Jordan and north of half tribe of Manasseh — 4.
    a. name; *b.* bound; *c.* characterize each territory.
3. *Regal period* — Saul to fall of the kingdom:
    (1) United under Saul, David and Solomen.
    (2) Divided at disruption of the kingdom.
    a. Judah — Benjamin, Judah and Simeon.
    b. Israel — remaining ten tribes.
    c. comparative size of the two territories.
4. *New Testament period* — under Rome:
    (1) west of Jordan: *a.* Galilee; *b.* Samaria; *c.* Judea; (2) east of Jordan: *a.* south of brook Hieromax, Perea; *b.* north of brook Hieromax, Bashan.
    a. bound; *b.* give principal cities; *c.* character of the country.

Draw an outline map of Palestine in each period. Locate the principal points and cities. Master these thoroughly.

Literature:

Hurlbut, Man. Bib. Geog., Map on p. 50, cf. p. 60.
" " p. 58.
" " pp. 64, 68, 100.
" " pp. 86, 88, 89.

§7. THE CHIEF POINTS AND CITIES IN PALESTINE.

1. *On sea coast:* *a.* Joppa; *b.* Carmel; *c.* Tyre; *a.* locate; *b.* give importance of each.
2. *On the mountain range:* *a.* Beersheba; *b.* Heron; *c.* Jerusalem; *d.* Bethel; *e.* Samaria; *f.* Shechem; *g.* Mt. Gilboa; *h.* Hazor.
3. *In the Jordan valley:* *a.* Jericho; *b.* Dan at sources of Jordan.
4. *On eastern table land:* *a.* Heshbon; *b.* Ramoth Gilead; *c.* Mahanaim.

Locate each of the above points in the divisions of Palestine in *a.* Patriarchal period; *b.* Tribal period; *c.* Regal period; *d.* N. T. period.

Make yourself master of the outlines and main points in Palestine before you leave them.

Literature:

Additional to preceding sections:
Osborn, Map of Palestine.
In Thomson's Land and Book.

1

Porter, Giant Cities of Bashan.
Each name in Smith's Bible Dictionary.
Any other trustworthy work on Palestine.

§8. JERUSALEM.

1. *Name:* a. in period of judges, Jebus, Judg. ix. 10; b. Jerusalem in Regal period; c. in Christian times, Holy City; d. now, El Khuds, 'the holy.'
2. *General location* (1) politically: a. territory of Jebusites; b. in Benjamin; c. in Judah; d. in Judea; (2) geographically: a. 32 miles from Mediterranean; b. 18 miles from Dead Sea; c. 20 miles north of Hebron; d. 36 miles south of Samaria; e. 2600 feet above sea level.
3. *Special location* — (1) Valleys uniting at S. E. angle of city: a. Hinnom, from N. W.; b. Kidron or Jehoshaphat from N.; c. Tyropœan from N. N. W.; (2) Mounts: a Zion S. W. between Hinnom and Tyropœan; b. Moriah S. E. between Tyropœan and Kidron; c, Acra N. of Zion; d. Bezetha N. of Moriah. Remark — a. Olivet is east of Jerusalem.
4. *Sections of the City*: a. upper city or Zion; b. lower city or Acra N. of Zion and W. of temple; c. Ophel, parks and gardens S. of Moriah; d. Moriah, N. of Ophel — contained the temple.

5. *History*: *a.* fortress of Jebusites until David's capture of it (1048); *b.* capital of United Kingdom, and of Judah; *c.* sacked by Shishak in Rehoboam's reign; *d.* sacked by Philistines and Arabians in reign of Jehoram; *e.* sacked by Joash of Israel in Amaziah's reign; *f.* sacked by Nebuchadrezzar in reign of Jehoiakim (608); *g.* sacked by same king in reign of Jehoiachin (599); *h.* sacked and destroyed by Neb. in reign of Zedekiah (588); *i.* rebuilt about 536–520; *j.* walls built by Nehemiah (445); *k.* sacked by Antiochus Epiphanes (168 B. C.); *l.* destroyed by the Romans in A. D., 70; *m.* at present a Turkish city of 20,000 inhabitants.

Literature:

Maps in Hurlbut, Man. Bib. Geog. pp. 72, 75, 78, 79, 81, 82.

Stanley, Sinai and Pal., p. 226. See also "Jerusalem" in index to Stanley.

Thomson, Land and Book, vol. 1, pp. 412–567. Admirable description, maps and cuts.

Fergusson, Ancient Topography of Jerusalem, 1847.

Williams, The Holy City, 2 vols., London, 1849.

Barclay, The City of the Great King. Phila., 1858.

Thrupp, Ancient Jerusalem, a new investigation, 1855.

Wilson and Warren, The Recovery of Jerusalem, New York, 1871.

Besant & Palmer, Jerusalem, the City of Herod and Saladin, new edition, London, 1889.

Sm. Bib. Dict., art. "Jerusalem."

III. LITERATURE.

§9. THE BOOKS OF THE BIBLE.

1. *In General.*
   1. The Bible contains *sixty-six* books.
      Isaiah contains *sixty-six* chapters.
   2. The Old Testament, *thirty-nine* books, is in general historical.
      The first section of Isaiah, *thirty-nine* chapters, is in general historical.
   3. The New Testament, *twenty-seven* books, is in general doctrinal.
      The Second section of Isaiah, *twenty-seven* chapters, is in general doctrinal or evangelical.
2. *The Books of the Old Testament.*
   1. Kinds of Literature in the Old Testament, historical, poetical, prophetical.
   2. Historical,   { Pentateuch   -   5
                     { Other hist. books   12
                                              ——
                                              17
   3. Poetical,   -   -   -   -   -   -   -   5
   4. Prophetical, -   - { Major Prophets   5
                           { Minor   "   12
                                              ——
                                              17
      Total,   -   -   -   -   -   -   39

§10. THE BOOKS AND CHAPTERS IN THE OLD TESTAMENT.

Commit to memory the entire list of books in the

Old Testament in their order, together with the number of chapters in each book. Follow the order under §9. 2. Observe a few points:

1. *In the Pentateuch:* Gen and Ex. contain chapters which are multiples of 10 (50 and 40); Lev. and Num. contain multiples of 9 (27 and 36).

2. *In the twelve other historical books:* a. Joshua and 2 Sam. contain each 24 chaps.; b. 1 Sam. contains same as Prov., 31 chaps.; c. 2 Chron. contains same as Num., 36 chaps.; d. Ezra and Esther contain each 10 chaps.

3. *Major Prophets:* Isaiah contains same number of chapters as the Bible does of books—*sixty-six.*

4. *Commit to memory the Minor Prophets.*

      Ho-Jo-Am Ob-Jo-Mi !
      Na-Ha-Ze
      Ha-Ze-Ma.

5. *In General.*

Three	chaps.	are	found	in	Joel, Nah , Hab. Zeph.
Four	"	"	"	"	Ruth, Jon. and Mal.
Ten	"	"	"	"	Ezra and Esther.
Twelve	"	"	"	"	Eccl. and Dan.
Fourteen	"	"	"	"	Hos. and Zech.
Twenty-four	"	"	"	"	Josh. and 1 Sam.
Thirty-one	"	"	"	"	2 Sam. and Prov.
Thirty-six	"	"	"	"	Num. and 2 Chron.

NOTE—Historical Books contain 436 chaps.
   Poetical " " 243 "
   Prophetical " " 250 "
     Total, - 929 "

i

§11. MODERATE GENERAL OUTFIT FOR THE STUDY OF OLD TESTAMENT HISTORY.†

Revised Version, minion, octavo. Oxford.
Hurlbut, Manual of Bib. Geography. Chicago.
Geikie, Hours with the Bible, either three or six volume edition. Potts, N. Y.
Blaikie, Manual of Bible History. Nelson, N. Y.
Josephus, Antiquities of the Jews.
Stanley, History of the Jewish Church, 3 vols. Scribner's, N. Y.
Thomson's The Land and the Book, 3 vols. Harpers, 1886.
*Edersheim, Bible History, 7 vols. London.
*Smith's Bible Dictionary, 4 vols.
*Smith's Old Testament History.
*By-Paths of Bible Knowledge, Religious Tract Soc., London.
*Bissell, Biblical Antiquities. Am. S. S. Union, 1888.
*Humphrey, E. P. Sacred History from Creation to Giving of the Law. New York, Armstrong, 1888.
*Men of the Bible Series, 10 vols. Randolph, N. Y.

Special works are cited in their appropriate places under *Literature*, at the end of each section.

---

†The unstarred works should be in the hands of every one; those starred are very useful and important, and should be consulted if possible.

IV. CHRONOLOGICAL.*

§12. PERIOD OF TIME COVERED BY THE BIBLE.

1. *The Old Testament describes peoples and events from 4004 to 400 B.C., or about 3,600 years.*
2. *The New Testament describes events from 4 B.C. to 100 A.D., or about 100 years.*
3. *Old Testament writings belong to a period from 1400 B.C. to 400 B.C., or about 1,000 years.*
4. *New Testament writings belong to a period from about 50 to 100 A.D., or about 50 years.*

---

* The chronology of Archbishop Ussher is adopted here *simply for the sake of convenience.* See Appendix.

§13. PERIODS OF OLD TESTAMENT HISTORY B. C.

This division seems to be a perfectly natural one, and such as will commend itself to the student.

i. *Ante-diluvian*, 4004–2348. Creation to the Deluge.
ii. *Post-diluvian*, 2348–1921. Deluge to the call of Abraham.
iii. *Patriarchal*, 1921–1706. Call of Abraham to the Descent into Egypt.
iv. *Bondage*, 1706–1491. Descent into Egypt to the Exodus.
v. *Wanderings*, 1491–1451. Exodus to Crossing of Jordan.
vi. *Conquest*, 1451–1400. Crossing of Jordan to Appointment of Judges.

1

vii. *Judges*, 1400–1095. Appointment of Judges to establishment of Kingdom.

viii. *Kingdom*, 1095–975. Establishment of Kingdom to Division of Kingdom.

ix. *Dual Kingdom*, 975–722. Division of Kingdom to Fall of Samaria.

x. *Judah alone*, 722–587. Fall of Samaria to Fall of Jerusalem.

xi. *Captivity—Exile*, 587–537. Fall of Jerusalem to Fall of Babylon.

xii. *Restoration*, 536–445. Fall of Babylon to the close of the Old Testament.

Remark.—Spare no pains to fix these periods firmly in mind. They are absolutely essential to a firm grasp of the outlines of Old Testament History.

1

SYLLABUS
OF THE
OUTLINES AND LITERATURE
OF
Old Testament History.

FIRST PERIOD.

ANTE-DILUVIAN. CREATION TO DELUGE.
B. C. 4004–2348.

§14. THE CREATION—GEN. I–II. 3.

1. *Analyze carefully by days Gen. i–ii. 3.*
2. *Give the work and progress in each day.*
3. *Ancient legends of Creation:* Geikie, vol. i. 3; Lenormant, chap. i.
4. *Meaning of God as used here.*
5. *Seventh day:* a. original significance; b. time indicated; c. relation to man's seventh day.
6. *Genesis and Geology—how far do they harmonize?* Geikie, vol. i. 4; Guyot; Dana's Review of Guyot.
7. *Age of the world:* Geikie, vol. i. 6.

8. *Object of Gen. i–ii. 3:* a. God is creator of all things; b. God prepared all things for man; c. God put man at the summit of creation; d. God pronounced him and all things "very good."
9. *Beginnings in this section:* a. solar system; b. all vegetable and animal life; c. man and woman; d. Sabbath.

Remark. — Learn carefully the work of each day, and note the threefold occurrence of "creation."

Literature:

Geikie, vol. i. chaps. 3–7.
Blaikie, Manual, chap. 1. secs. 2 and 3.
Edersheim, Bible History, vol. i. chap. 1.
Humphrey, Sacred History, chap. 2.
Lenormant, Beginnings of History, chap. 1.
Guyot, Creation, and review of same by Prof. Dana in Bib. Sac., vol. xlii. pp. 201–224.
"Creation" in Smith's Bib. Dic. and McClintock & Strong's Encyc.
Bibliotheca Sacra, vols. xii. p. 61 sq., 323 sq.; xiv, p. 75 sq.; xxiv. p. 434 sq.; xxvii. p. 459 sq.
Prof. Dana in Bib. Sac., vol. xiii. pp. 80–130, 631–655; vol. xiv. pp. 388–413, 461–525, 854–874.
Prof. Dana in Old and New Test. Student, July and August, 1890.
Miller, Hugh, Testimony of the Rocks, secs. 3 and 4.

i

§15. EDEN — GEN. II. 4–25.

1. *Analyze Gen. ii. 4–25.*
2. *Is this a second account of creation?* Lenormant chap. 1.
3. *Creation of man in distinction from that of animals:* a. image of God; b. dominion on the earth; c. has breath of life, a living soul.
4. *Traditions of man's creation:* Geikie, vol. i. 8; Lenormant.
5. *Antiquity of man :* Geikie, vol. i. 9, 10.
6. *Location of Eden*—Bible account. Other views: a. Armenia; c. Babylonia; e. near Damascus; d. North pole.
7. *Occupation of Adam:* a. body; b. mind; c. soul.
8. *Adam and Eve — woman:* Geikie, vol. i. 7.
9. *Object of this account:* a. give more completely the relation of man to his maker; b. the relation of man to the animal world; c. the relations of man and woman.

Literature:

Geikie, Hours, vol. i. chaps. 8–11.
Blaikie, Manual, chap. 1, secs. 4 and 5.
Edersheim, Bible History, vol. i. chap. 1.
Humphrey, Sacred History, chap. 3.
Lenormant, Beginnings, chap. 2.
Delitzsch, Wo lag das Paradies? Leipzig, 1881.
Engel, M., Loesung der Paradieses Frage, Leipzig, 1885.

Warren, W. F., Paradise Found: the Cradle of the Human Race at the North Pole. Boston, 1885.

Brown, Francis, Old and New Test. Student. Sept., 1884.

Gibson, The Ages before Moses. N. Y., 1879.

§ 16. THE TEMPTATION AND THE FALL—GEN. III.

1. *Analysis of Gen. iii:* *a.* serpent through the tree of good and evil deceives Adam and Eve, vss. 1–6; *b.* awakening of shame, 7, 8; *c.* examination of God, 9–13; *d.* judgment given, 14–19; *e.* Eve named; *f.* the two clothed; *g.* expulsion from the garden.
2. *The serpent* (symbolism in O. and N. T., 2 Cor. xi. 3; Gen. xlix. 17; Rev. xii. 9; xx. 2): *a.* his plan; *b.* his success.
3. *Sin of Adam and Eve, what was it?* *a.* mythical interpretation; *b.* allegorical interpretation; *c.* historical interpretation.
4. *Punishment, what kind of death was it?*
5. *Immediate punishment:* *a.* serpent — cursed; *b.* Eve — sorrow in childbirth and subjection to her husband; *c.* Adam — hard work, return to dust.
6. *Traditions of this sin among other nations:* Lenormant, chap. 3.
7. *Deliverance in the distant future, iii.* 15: from the seed of a *woman* shall the bruiser arise.

i

8. *Cherubim in the Old Testament — symbolism:* Ex. xxv. 17–22; Ps. lxxx. 1; Ezek. xxviii. 14; ix. 3; x. 18.
9. *Flaming sword—symbolism:* Isa. xxxiv. 5; Jer. xlvi. 10; Zeph. ii. 12.
10. *Beginnings in chap. iii:* *a.* disobedience, sin; *b.* enmity; *c.* cursing; *d.* sorrow; *e.* toil; *f.* physical death; *g.* clothing; *h.* promise of a redeemer.

Literature:

Geikie, Hours, vol. i. chap. 11.
Edersheim, Bible History, vol. i. chap. 1.
Humphrey, Sacred History, chaps. 4 and 5.
Lenormant, Beginnings, chap. 3. .
Expositor's Bible, Genesis, chap. ii.
Genesis of Sin, Princeton Review, July, '80.
Edenic Period of Man,   "   "   "   "
First Sin, Contemp. Review, September, '79.
Art. *Sin*, Dicts. and Encycs.

§17. CAIN AND HIS DESCENDANTS—GEN. IV.

1. *Analyze Gen. iv.*
2. *Compare the offerings of Cain and Abel.*
3. *Cain's wrath and murder of Abel:* *a.* countenance fallen; *b.* rebuked by Jehovah; *c.* slays Abel.
4. *Significance in history* (cf. Gen. ix. 5; Job xvi. 18; Isa. xxvi. 21): *a.* culmination of Eve's disobedience, of Cain's formalism, jealousy and

wrath; *b.* first murder—mutilation of God's creature.

5. *Punishment of Cain:* *a.* denial of any knowledge of Abel; *b.* cursed by Jehovah; *c.* fugitive and vagabond in the earth; *d.* sign set on him to save his life; *e.* sin at the door (cf. Prov. ix. 14; xxviii. 17).

6. *Traditions of similar murder among other peoples.* See Lenormant.

7. *Lamech and the origin of the arts:* *a.* nomads and shepherds; *b.* musical instruments; *c.* cutting instruments (of war and agriculture).

8. *Lamech's song:* *a.* earliest specimen of Hebrew poetry; *b.* first case of polygamy; *c.* intimations of violence in the land.

9. *Birth of Seth:* cf. Cain's descendants with those of Seth in Gen. v.

10. *Beginnings in Chapter iv:* *a.* sacrifice-offering; *b.* murder; *c.* city; *d.* arts; *e.* poetry; *f.* polygamy; *g.* calling upon God.

Literature:

Geikie, Hours, vol. i. chap. 12.
Edersheim, Bible History, vol. i. chap. 2.
Humphrey, Sacred History, chap. 6.
Smith, Old Test. History, chap. 4.
Lenormant, Beginnings, chaps. 4 and 5.
Expositor's Bible, Genesis.
Articles, *Cain, Abel* and *Lamech* in Smith's Bible Dictionary.

§18. SETH AND HIS DESCENDANTS—GEN. V.

1. *Analyze Gen. v.*
2. *Compare carefully the descendants of Cain and Seth.* See Lenormant, iv.
3. *Similar genealogies among other peoples.* See Lenormant.
4. *Variations in the periods of time between Adam and the Deluge:* a. Hebrew 1656 years; b. Samaritan 1307 years; c. Septuagint 2242 years; d. explanations of these differences.
5. *Longevity of the antediluvians:* a. between Adam and Noah men lived 200–600 years (Gen. xi. 10–32); b. Mosaic and patriarchal times, 100–200 years (Gen. xx. 7; xxxv. 28; xlvii. 28); e. later O. T. times, 70–80 years.
6. *Various interpretations of these facts.*
7. *Translation of Enoch* (cf. Isa. xvii. 14; Ps. ciii. 16); cf. Apocryphal *Book of Enoch.*

Literature:

Geikie, Hours, vol. i, chap. 12.
Blaikie, Manual, chap. 2, sec. 1.
Edersheim, Bible History, vol. i. chaps. 3 and 4.
Humphrey, Sacred Hist., chaps. 6 and 7.
Lenormant, Beginnings, chap. 6.
The Book of Enoch, translation by Schodde.
Articles *Chronology, Enoch,* in Smith's Bib. Dict.
Antediluvians, Longevity, Patriarch, in McClintock & Strong's Encyc.

SECOND PERIOD.

POST-DILUVIAN. DELUGE TO CALL OF ABRAHAM. B.C. 2348–1921.

§19. THE DELUGE—GEN. VII–VIII. 14.

1. *Cause—wickedness in the earth:* a. "Sons of God and daughters of men," three views, (1) sons of princes and daughters of lower orders, (2) angels and mankind generally, (3) Sethites or godly men and Cainites; b. "My spirit shall not rule in man forever," 2 Peter ii. 5; c. repentance of God (cf. 1 Sam. xv. 29), grief or pain on account of sin.
2. *Ark:* a. dimensions; b. material; c. shape; d. possibility of containing all to be saved.
3. *Time of entering and contents.*
4. *Beginning and duration of deluge*: 40 days, 150 days, 360 days.
5. *Universality of deluge—arguments pro and con:* consider that *the earth* was (1) Palestine alone, Joel i. 2; Ps. xliv. 3; (2) a small district about a town, Josh. viii. 1; (3) indefinite, "every nation under heaven," Acts ii. 5; (4) "throughout the whole [known] world," Rom. i. 8.
6. *Object of the deluge:* destruction of wicked men only.

7. *Are there two Biblical accounts of the deluge?* See Lenormant.
8. *Babylonian account—differs how from the Bible?*
9. *Other traditions:* a. Indian; b. Greek; c. Iranian; d. Cymrics; e. Scandinavian; f. Lithuanian.

Literature:

Geikie, Hours, vol. i. chaps. 13 and 14.
Blaikie, Manual, chap. 2, secs. 1 and 2.
Edersheim, Bible History, vol. i. chaps. 5 and 6.
Humphrey, Sacred History, chaps. 7 and 8.
Lenormant, Beginnings, chaps. 7 and 8; and Appendix v.
Articles, *Deluge* in Encyc. Brit.; *Noah* in Smith's Bib. Dict.
Expositor's Bible, Genesis.
Geikie, O. T. Characters, on *Noah*.

§20. THE SECOND BEGINNING—GEN. VIII. 15—IX.

1. *Events immediately upon landing:* a. first altar; b. sacrifice; c. divine promise; d. blessing; e. command to multiply.
2. *All living things put under man's surveillance:* a. to command; b. to use for food.
3. *Capital punishment established, blood for blood.*
4. *Covenant on God's part:* a. not to cut off all life again with a flood; b. not to bring another flood upon the earth.
5. *Noah's shame and prophecy.*

6. *Canaan's curse*—(cf. 1 Kings ix. 20-21.)
7. *Shem's future.*
8. *Japheth's part in Shem's God.*
9. *Beginnings in this section:* a. new race; b. altar; b. bloody sacrifice; c. capital punishment; d. flesh for food; f. promise by nature—bow in the cloud; g. drunkenness; h. prediction by man.

Literature:

Geikie, Hours, vol. i. chap. 15.
Blaikie, Manual, chap. ii. sec. 4.
Edersheim, Bible History, vol. i. chap. **6**.
Humphrey, Sacred History, chap. 9.
Briggs Messianic Prophecy.
Orelli, Old Testament Prophecy.
Expositor's Bible, Genesis, chap. 6.
Geikie, O. T. Characters, on *Noah.*
Denio, F. B. The Rainbow in Genesis, Old and New Test. Student, May 1890.

§21. THE TABLE OF NATIONS—GEN. X.

The most complete and exact table known.

1. *Does it speak of individuals or of nations?* a. sons=tribe; b. used here in pl.; c. single names used as *nations* in Bible, in Ezek. xxvii. 7-15; xxxviii. 2-6.
2. *Is it geographical or ethnographical?*
3. *Locate and identify the sons of Japheth:* a. Armenia; b. Asia Minor; c. Greece in Europe.

4. *Locate and identify the sons of Ham:* a.* Cush, S. Babylonia, Arabian peninsula south, upper Nile; b. Mizraim, N. Egypt, coast of Mediterranean Sea; c. Put—Punt, modern province of Hejaz; d. Canaan, E. coast of Mediterranean in Asia, Phœnicians, Canaanites, Hittites, etc.
5. *Locate and identify the sons of Shem:* a. Elam =highland, with capital at Shushan; b. Asshur, Assyria, cf. vs. 11; c. Arpachshad, between Lakes Van and Urumiyeh, settled in upper Babylonia and Mesopotamia, ancestors of Hebrews; d. Lud, Lydians in Asia Minor; e. Aram, Harran, Hamath, N. Mesopotamia to Upper Syria, later a general term for Armenia, Taurus, Lebanon, N. Palestine. Arabian Desert on S. and Euphrates and Tigris on the East.
6. *Source and directions of early migrations:* From Central Asia, E., W. and S.
7. *Scientific evidences of racial affinity:* a. language; b. physiognomy; c. physiology; d. psychology; e. religious nature.

Literature:

Geikie, Hours, vol. i. chap. 16.
Blaikie, Manual, chap. 3, sec. 1.
Edersheim, Bible History, vol. i. chap. 8.

*NOTE—Nimrod, first founder of a mighty empire. (Hunter—Assyrian kings hunted their enemies cf. Mic. v. 6.) a. A Cushite; b. settled in Shinar; c. extended his empire northwards.

Humphrey, Sacred History, chaps. 10 and 12.
Hurlbut, Man. of Bib. Geog., pp. 23–27.
Smith, O. T. History, chap. v.
Schrader, E., Cuneiform Inscriptions and the Old Testament, pp. 61–103.
Thomson's Land and Book.
Also Dictionaries and Encyclopedias under the various names.
Commentaries on Genesis x.

§22. THE TOWER OF BABEL AND THE DISPERSION — GEN. XI. 1–9.

1. *Analyze the Biblical account.*
2. *Locate the event:* a. Shinar; b. where bricks were used for stone; c. Babylonia.
3. *Purpose of the tower:* a. safety against another deluge; b. national headquarters; c. idolatrous centre.
4. *God's means of frustrating their purpose:* a. lightning; b. confusion — disease of the mouth(?); c. scattering.
5. *What was the sin of the tower-builders?*
6. *Traditions among other peoples:* Egypt, Babylon, Greece.
7. *Relation of Babel to "Birs Nimroud:"* See Rawlinson.
8. *Were all languages originally one?*
9. *Was the origin of different languages due to a miracle?*

i

Literature:

Geikie, Hours, vol. i. chap. 17.
Blaikie, Manual, chap. 3, sec. 12.
Edersheim, Bible History, vol. i. chap. 8.
Humphrey, Sacred History, chap. 11.
Schrader, Cun. Inscrip. and O. T., pp. 103–114.
Smith, O. T. History, chap. 5.
Kurtz, Hist. of Old Covenant, pp. 108–122.
Rawlinson, Ancient Monarchies, vol. i. p. 21, for *Birs Nimroud*
Tongues, Confusion of, in Smith's Bib. Dictionary.

THIRD PERIOD.

PATRIARCHAL. CALL OF ABRAHAM TO DESCENT INTO EGYPT. B. C. 1921–1706.

§23. ABRAHAM'S CALL AND WANDERINGS—GEN. XI. 10—XIII. 18.

1. *Descendant of Shem*—xi. 10–26.
2. *First remove, from Ur of Chaldees*—xi. 27–32: *a.* location; *b.* population; *c.* associates; *d.* religion, Josh. xxiv. 2, 14.
3. *Second remove, from Haran*—xii. 1–4: *a.* location; *b.* associates; *c.* promise of God.
4. *First journey through Canaan*—xii. 5–9: *a* builds altar in Shechem, promise to Abraham's seed; *b.* Bethel, an altar built, calls on the name of Jehovah; *c.* South country.
5. *Sojourning in Egypt*—xii. 10–20: *a.* famine drives him thence; *b.* deception of Pharaoh; *c.* plagues on Pharaoh; *d.* Abraham treated kindly—why?
6. *Return to Canaan*—xiii. 1–4: *a.* companions and wealth; *b.* South country; *c.* Bethel, old altar, calls of Jehovah.
7. *Separation of Abraham and Lot*—xiii. 5 sq. *a.* greatness of herds; *b.* strife of herdsmen; *c.* Lot

/

takes circle of Jordan; *d.* Abraham takes Canaan (probably the hill-country); *e.* promise repeated to Abraham; *f.* Abraham removes to Oaks of Mamre, builds an altar there.
8. *Contemporaneous history: a.* Ur of Chaldees; *b.* at Haran; *c.* in Canaan; *d.* in Egypt.

Literature:

Geikie, Hours, vol. i. 18, 19, 20, 21.
Blaikie, Manual, chap. 4, sec. 1.
Edersheim, Bible History, vol. i. chaps. 10 and 11.
Humphrey, Sacred History, chaps. 13–15.
Stanley, Jewish Church, Lecs. 1 and 2.
Hurlbut, Man. of Bib. Geog., pp. 33–35.
Tomkins, Times of Abraham.
Mozley, Lectures on O. T., Lec. 1.
Deane, W. J., Life and Times of Abraham, Men of Bible series.
Geikie, O. T. Characters, *Abraham.*
Each name in Bib. Dict. and Encycs.

§24. ABRAHAM'S SETTLED LIFE IN CANAAN—GEN. XIV—XXIII.

1. *Invasion by the kings of the East*—xiv. 1-17: *a.* subdued territory; *b.* years of subjection and revolt; *c.* territory invaded; *d.* disaster to the cities of the plain; *e.* Abraham's pursuit and victory.
2. *Melchizedek*—xiv. 18–20: *a.* office; *b.* blessing upon Abraham; *c.* tithe observed (origin?); *d.* who was Melchizedek?—cf. Heb. vii. 1–11.

3. *Abraham's vision*—xv: *a.* seed to be as stars of heaven; *b.* believed Jehovah—righteousness, vs. 6; *c.* sacrifice and vision, seed in bondage 400 years; *d.* to possess from river of Egypt to the great river.

4. *Story of Hagar*—xvi: *a.* Egyptian hand-maid; *b.* flees to the wilderness; *c.* first mention of the *Angel of Jehovah*—promise to Hagar; *d.* return and birth of Ishmael.

5. *Renewed promise and rite of circumcision*—xvii—xviii. 15: *a.* great seed and possession of Canaan; *b.* rite of circumcision established in Israel, (found among other peoples?); *c.* appearance of three angels, their errand.

6. *Fate of Sodom*—xviii. 16—xix. 38: *a.* announced by three angels; *b.* Abraham's plea; *c.* two angelic guests of Lot; *d.* Sodomites charge on his house, blindness; *e.* early escape of Lot and family; *f.* fate of Lot's wife; *g.* city destroyed by fire and brimstone (explain); *h.* Lot's incestuous posterity.

7. *Abraham and Abimelech*—xx—xxi. 21: *a.* Abraham deceives Abimelech; *b.* Abimelech's vision; *c.* kind treatment of Abraham; *d.* birth of Isaac; *e.* expulsion of Hagar and Ishmael; *f.* distress of Hagar; *g.* covenant between Abraham and Abimelech; *h.* origin of Beer-sheba.

8. *Sacrifice of Isaac*—xxii: *a.* to prove Abraham; *b.* journey; *c.* locality (Moriah); *d.* tragedy averted by substitute; *e.* promise renewed.

NOTE—Human sacrifices, prevalence in Old Test. times; cf. Sunday School Times, Feb. 19, 1887; Mozley, Lec. 3; Kalisch. Com. on Lev. i. pp. 323-396.

9. *Death and burial of Sarah*—xxiii: *a.* aged 127 years; *b.* Abraham bought the cave of Macpelah from a Hittite; *c.* Sarah buried therein.
10. *Character of Abraham:* *a.* faithful to God and man; *b.* skilled in business; *c.* self-possessed and generous; *d.* exemplary patriarch in every way.
11. *Contemporaneous History:* *a.* in the East; *b.* Hittites; *c.* Philistines.

Literature:

Geikie, Hours, vol. i. chap. 22.
Blaikie, Manual, chap. 4, sec. 1.
Edersheim, Bible History, vol. i. chaps. 12–14.
Humphrey, Sacred History, chaps. 16–21.
Stanley, Jewish Church, Lecs. 1 and 2 in part.
Cun. Inscrip. and Old Test., pp. 120–123.
Mozley, Lectures on Old Test., Lecs. 2 and 3.
Meyer, F. B., Abraham; or the Obedience of Faith, Revell, Chicago, 1890.

§25. CAREER OF ISAAC—GEN. XXIV—XXVIII. 9; XXXV. 28.

1. *Finding of Rebekah*—xxiv: *a.* oath of the servant; *b.* journey to Mesopotamia; *c.* kin of

Nahor, Abraham's brother; *d.* return with Rebekah; she meets Isaac.

2. *Last days of Abraham*—xxv. 1–11: *a.* another wife and posterity; *b.* death and burial in Macpelah.

3. *Isaac's sons, Jacob and Esau*—xxv. 12–34; xxvi. 34, 35: *a.* character of the boys; *b.* birthright of Esau sold to Jacob; *c.* Esau's wives—Hittites.

4. *Isaac in Gerar*—xxvi: *a.* famine in Canaan; *b.* Jehovah's promise, warned against Egypt; *c.* deceives men of Gerar; *d.* strife over the wells at Gerar; *e.* oath and peace.

5. *Isaac's blessing stolen by Jacob*—xxvii: *a.* Isaac's request for venison; *b.* Rebekah's intrigue for Jacob; *c.* Jacob's success and blessing; *d.* Esau's grief; *e.* Jacob sent to Paddan-aram for a wife.

6. *Isaac's death and burial*—xxxv. 28, 29: *a.* after Jacob's return; *b.* buried by both Jacob and Esau.

7. *Isaac's character:* *a.* faith in God; *b.* retiring; *c.* not forceful; *d.* submissive, peaceful.

Literature:

Geikie, Hours, vol. i. chap. 23.
Blaikie, Manual, chap. 4, sec. 2.
Edersheim, Bible History, vol. i. chaps. 15 and 16.
Humphrey, Sacred History, chaps. 22 and 23.
Stanley, Jewish Church, Lec. 2, last part.

Geikie, Old Test. Characters, on *Isaac* and *Ishmael*.
Dods; Isaac, Jacob and Joseph, London, 1887.

§26. THE WANDERINGS OF JACOB TO THE STORY OF JOSEPH—GEN. XXVIII. 10—XXXV. 27.

1. *Flight to Haran*—xxviii. 10-22: *a.* vision at Bethel; *b.* pillar set up; *c.* vow to Jehovah —tithe.
2. *Sojourn with Laban, his uncle*—xxix. 1—xxxi. 16: *a.* shepherd; *b.* service for Rachel and Leah; *c.* Laban's deceit; *d.* Jacob's children, (xxxv. 23-26); *e.* Jacob's shrewdness in caring for the flock; *f.* his wealth.
3. *Jacob's flight from Laban*—xxxi. 17-55: *a.* unawares, he leaves with his all; *b.* pursuit by Laban; *c.* Jacob overtaken in Gilead; *d.* vain search for the teraphim; *e.* "heap of witness" set up; *f.* peaceful separation.
4. *Esau ahead*—xxxii—xxxiii. 17: *a.* messengers to Esau; *b.* their return, report, and prayer of Jacob; *c.* present sent to Esau; *d.* division of families and flocks; *e.* wrestling with the angel at Penuel and Jacob named Israel; *f.* joyful meeting with Esau; *g.* Esau receives presents and returns in peace.

NOTE—Esau's posterity is given in chap. xxxvi.

5. *Jacob at Shechem*—xxxiii. 18—xxxiv. 31: *a.* bought ground; *b.* built an altar; *c.* Dinah disgraced; *d.* design of Jacob's sons, and despoiling of Shechem.

6. *Jacob at Bethel*—xxxv. 1–20: *a.* all strange gods to be put away; *b.* Bethel reached; *c.* Deborah dies; *d.* renewed promise; *e.* birth of Benjamin and death of Rachel on way to Ephrath.
7. *Characteristics of Jacob and Esau.*
8. *Contrast the characters of Abraham and Jacob.*
9. *Give outline of Jacob's journeyings.*

Literature:

Geikie, Hours, vol. i. chap. 23 and half of 24.
Blaikie, Manual, chap. 4, sec. 3.
Edersheim, Bible History, vol. i. chaps. 16–18.
Humphrey, Sacred History, chaps. 24 and 25.
Stanley, Jewish Church, Lec. 3.
Smith, O. T. History, chap. 8.
Geikie, Old Test. Characters, on *Jacob*, *Esau*, *Leah and Rachel*, *Judah*.
Meyer, F. B., Israel, a Prince with God, Revell, Chicago, 1890.
Names in Bible Dicts. and Encycs.

§27. JACOB AND JOSEPH TO DESCENT INTO EGYPT —GEN. XXXVII—XLV.

1. *Joseph's sale to the Midianites*—xxxvii: *a.* age of Joseph; *b.* Joseph's two dreams; *c.* visit to his brethren; *d.* disposal of him, pit, sale; *e.* caravan routes.
2. *Judah's unfaithfulness*—xxxviii.
3. *Joseph sold and imprisoned*—xxxix. xl: *a.* slave

1

of Potiphar; *b.* his favor; *c.* falsely charged and imprisoned; *d.* favor in prison; *e.* interprets dream of butler and baker—fulfilled.

4. *Joseph's release and promotion*, xli : *a.* interprets Pharaoh's dreams; *b.* becomes *second* officer in the kingdom; *c.* charge of crops, storehouses; *d.* marries daughter of an Egyptian priest; *e.* famine on hand.
5. *Jacob's distress and appeal to Egypt*, xlii — xlv: *a.* ten sons go to Egypt for corn; *b.* rough reception and return; *c.* second trip with Benjamin; *d.* feast and favor at Joseph's hands; *e.* return hindered by intrigue; *f.* Judah's matchless plea; *g.* Joseph reveals himself; *h.* arrangements for transfer to to Egypt of Jacob's house.
6. *Egypt before the Hebrew sojourn:* Geikie, vol. ii. 2: *a.* early history; *b.* religion; *c.* political relations.

Literature:

Geikie, Hours, vol. i. chap. 24.
Blaikie, Manual, chap. 4, sec. 4.
Edersheim, Bible History, vol. i. chaps. 19–21.
Humphrey, Sacred History, chap. 26.
Stanley, Jewish Church, Lec. 4 in part.
Geikie, Old Test. Characters, on *Joseph*.
Kellogg, A. H., Abraham, Moses and Joseph in Egypt. N. Y., 1887.

FOURTH PERIOD.

BONDAGE. DESCENT INTO EGYPT TO THE EXODUS. B. C. 1706–1491.

§28. DESCENT AND SETTLEMENT IN EGYPT—GEN. XL—L.

1. *Journey to Egypt*, xlvi: *a.* renewed promise; *b.* number who went down; *c.* meeting of Israel and Joseph.
2. *Pharaoh's favor to Israel*, xlvii—xlviii: *a.* assigned to Goshen; *b.* Joseph's authority; *c.* Israel's age; *d.* Joseph's sons blessed by Israel.
3. *Egypt:* Hurlbut, Man. Bib. Geog., pp. 41, 42: *a.* boundaries; *b.* extent; *c.* characteristics; *d.* history.
4. *Land of Goshen*, Geikie, vol. ii. chap. 1: *a.* location; *b.* size; *c.* seasons; *d.* products.
5. *Israel's prophecy in regard to his twelve sons*, xlix. 1–27: characterize each son.
6. *Israel's death*, xlix. 28—l. 13: *a.* command for burial; *b.* embalmed; *c.* caravan to Canaan; *d.* buried in Macpelah; *e.* fear of Joseph's brethren.
7. *Joseph's death*, l. 15–26 *a.* prophecy; *b.* death; *c.* embalming.
8. *Character of Joseph.*

i

Literature:

Geikie, Hours, vol. i. chap. 24 in part; vol. ii. chap. 1.
Blaikie, Manual, chap. 5, sec. 1.
Edersheim, Bib. History, vol. i. chap. 22 and 23; vol. ii. chap. 1.
Humphrey, Sacred History, chap. 27.
Stanley, Jewish Church, Lec. 4, i.
Smith, Old Test. History, chap. 10.
Hurlbut, Man Bib. Geog., pp. 41 and 42.

§29. THE SOJOURN IN EGYPT—EXODUS I–X.

1. *Reigning power in Egypt at this time:* a. at descent of Jacob; b. after death of Joseph.
2. *Religion of Egypt:* a. nature worship; b. extensive ritual; c. numerous priesthood.
3. *Servitude of Israel*, i. 8—ii. 10: a. beginning, due to what? b. what kinds of work? c. attempted suppression of increase; d. Moses' preservation, attempted deliverance and flight to Midian.
4. *Moses' training*, ii. 11—iv. 18: a. among the flocks of Jethro; b. bush of flaming fire; c. command of Jehovah for Israel; d. two signs to Moses of success; e. Aaron's help assured.
5. *Moses' return and first appeal to Pharaoh*, iv. 18—vii. 13: a. events on the way back; b. Moses and Aaron's vain appeal to Pharaoh; c. increase of the burdens—bricks without straw; d. Jehovah's assurance of success; e. signs before Pharaoh—rods, explain.

6. *First nine plagues,* vii. 14–x. 29: A.(*1*) blood—no effect; (*2*) frogs—Pharaoh calls; (*3*) lice—no effect; (*4*) flies—Pharaoh calls; (*5*) murrain—no effect; (*6*) boils—no effect; (*7*) hail—Pharaoh calls; (*8*) locusts—Pharaoh calls; (*9*) darkness—Pharaoh calls.

B. Observe: *a.* Pharaoh calls for Moses and Aaron five times; *b.* Pharaoh's heart is hard (obstinate) in (1), (3) and (5); *c.* Pharaoh made hard his heart in (2), (4) and (7); *d.* Jehovah hardened his heart in (6), (8) and (9) only; *e.* concessions of Pharaoh after (4), (7), (8) and (9); *f.* natural explanations for these plagues? *g.* gods insulted by each plague?

Literature:

Geikie, Hours, vol. ii. chaps. 3–5.
Blaikie, Manual, chap. v. secs. 2 and 3.
Edersheim, Bible History, vol. ii. chaps. 2–6.
Humphrey, Sacred Hist., chaps. 28–31.
Stanley, Jewish Church, Lec. 4 in part.
Hurlbut, Man. Bib. Geog., pp. 41, 42.
Stanley, Sinai and Palestine, Introduction.
Rawlinson, Life and Times of Moses, Men of Bible Series.
Harper, H. A., Bible and Modern Discoveries. Boston, 1889.
Renouf, Religion of Egypt, London, 1879.
Geikie, Old Test. Characters, on *Pharaoh, Pharaoh's Daughter, Moses, Aaron.*

i

FIFTH PERIOD.

WANDERINGS. EXODUS TO CROSSING THE JORDAN. B. C. 1491–1451.

§30. THE EXODUS. EXODUS XI–XV, 21.

1. *Preliminary to the tenth plague,* xi: *a.* asking of Egyptians, why? *b.* threat told to Israel; *c.* result foretold.
2. *Passover established,* xii. 1-28, 42-51; xiii. 1–10: *a.* times set—first month of year, tenth day; *b.* preparation of lamb, on 14th day; *c.* disposal of the blood; *d.* purpose of same; *e.* manner of eating; *f.* exact time of eating; *g.* memorial to be observed; *h.* typical significance.
3. *The tenth plague,* xii. 29–36; *a.* at midnight; *b.* first-born of man and beast slain; *c.* call of Pharaoh for Moses and Aaron; *d.* command to Israel to leave; *e.* they start — spoiling Egyptians.
4. *The march to the sea,* xii. 37—xiv. 14; *a.* assembling of hosts of Israel; *b.* journey from Rameses to Succoth—600,000 *men,* armed; *c.* sanctification of first-born; *d.* bones of Joseph with them; *e.* from Succoth to Etham; *f.* fire and pillar of cloud; *g.* before

Pi-hahiroth, between Migdol and the sea, before Baal Zephon; *h.* Pharaoh's pursuit—600 chariots; *i.* Israel's cry to Jehovah.

5. *The crossing*, xiv. 15–31: *a.* assurance of deliverance; *b.* pillar between the two camps; *c.* Moses' rod over the sea; *d.* all night wind drove back the waters; *e.* Israel passes over on dry land; *f.* fatal result to the Egyptians; *g.* Israel's strengthened belief in Jehovah.
6. *The route or place of crossing* (see Harper, Bible and Modern Disc.): *a.* not in N. as advocated formerly by Brugsch; *b.* not at present N. end of Red Sea; *c.* but probably at Lake Menzaleh; *d.* three days from Elim.
7. *Moses' Song*, xv. 1–21: *a.* analyze it carefully; *b.* chief thought; *c.* references to outside peoples; *d.* purpose of the song.
8. *Contemporaneous history:* *a.* waning of Egypt's power; *b.* revolts of their foreign dependencies; *c.* advantage to Israel of these things.
9. *Effects of Bondage on Israel.* See Blaikie, chap. v., sec. 5.

Geikie, Hours, vol. ii., chap. 6.
Blaikie, Manual, chap. v., secs. 4 and 5.
Edersheim, Bible History, vol. ii., chap. 7.
Humphrey, Sacred History, chap. 32.
Stanley, Jewish Church, Lec. 5.
Rawlinson, Life and Times of Moses.
Geikie, Old Test. Characters, on *Moses, Aaron, Miriam.*

i

Harper, H. A., Bible and Modern Disc., pp. 77–177.
Brugsch, H., The Route of the Exodus. And numerous articles in reviews and magazines.
Ebers, George, Durch Gosen zum Sinai. Leipzig, 1872.
Birks, T. R., The Exodus of Israel. London, 1863.
Hengstenberg, E. W., Egypt and the Books of Moses. Andover, 1843.

§31. THE MARCH TO SINAI—EX. XV. 22—XVIII. 27.

1. *The wilderness:* a. location, boundary, size; b. natural features; c. inhabitants, then and today.
2. *Numbers, condition and spirit of Israel.*
3. *Halts at Marah and Elim*, xv. 22–27. a. travel through Shur (wall); b. bitter water made sweet at Marah; c. covenant of Jehovah there; d. Elim.
4. *In the wilderness of Sin*, xvi. 1–36; a. arrival on 15th day of 2d month; b. murmur of Israel against Moses; c. Jehovah's reply; d. quails in evening—whence? e. manna in morning—its character; f. regulations for gathering it.
5. *In Rephidim*, xvii. 1—xviii. 27: a. no water; b. strife of people with Moses; c. Horeb smitten—water; d. Amalek defiant; e. Israel under Joshua victorious; f. fate of Amalek pronounced.

6. *Jethro*, xviii. 1–27: *a.* father-in-law to Moses; *b.* Jethro recognizes Jehovah as great; *c.* advises division of labor; *d.* Moses follows advice.
7. *Ancient modes of travel.*

Literature:

Geikie, Hours, vol. ii. chaps. 7 and 8.
Blaikie, Manual, chap. 6, sec. 1.
Edersheim, Bible History, vol. ii. chaps. 7 and 8.
Stanley, Jewish Church, Lec. 6.
" Sinai and Palestine, Part I.
Hurlbut, Man. Bib. Geog., pp. 40–45.
Rawlinson, Moses his Life and Times.
Bartlett, Forty Days in the Desert.
Palmer, The Desert of the Exodus, 2 vols.
Wilson, The Lands of the Bible, vol. i.
Gage, Studies in Bible Lands.
Wallace, The Desert and the Holy Land.

§32. DOINGS AT SINAI IN BOOK OF EXODUS— XIX–XL.

1. *Site of Sinai, time of arrival, and distance from Egypt?* xix. 1, 2.
2. *First doings*, xix. 3–25: *a.* Jehovah appears to Moses in mount; *b.* people covenant with Jehovah; *c.* Jehovah appears to Moses in mount second time; *d.* people sanctified by Moses; *e.* thunderings the third day; *f.* Jehovah appears to Moses third time in the mount; *g.* gives charge to the people.

3. *Ten Commandments*, xx. 2–17; *a.* spoken *directly* to the people; *b.* analyze the commandments; *c.* compare them with Deut. v. 6–21; *d.* fear of the people; *e.* Moses to be the mediator between Israel and Jehovah.
4. *Minor laws*, xxi—xxiii. 13, 18–33. *a.* servants; *b.* manslaughter; *c.* stealing; *d.* unintentional acts; *e.* idolatry, etc., etc.
5. *The feasts*, xxiii. 14–17 ; *Lev.* xxii ; *Num.* xxviii–xxx: *a.* unleavened bread or passover —time? *b.* first-fruits, or pentecost, or weeks, or wheat harvest—time? *c.* ingatherings or tabernacles — time? *d.* give significance of each.
6. *Moses*, xxiv: *a.* builds an altar; *b.* offers up offerings; *c.* forty days and nights in the mount, fourth ascent; *d.* leaves the people with Aaron and Hur.
7. *Tent of meeting*, *Ex.* xxv—xxxi., xxxv—xl: (1) Tabernacle. I. Holy of Holies: *a.* ark; *b.* mercy seat; *c.* cherubim. II. Holy place: *a.* altar of incense; *b.* table and vessels; *c.* candlestick and vessels. III. Court: *a.* great altar; *b.* laver of brass. (2) Priests' garments. (3) Oil of anointing. (4) dedication: *a.* time; *b.* services; *c.* cloud and glory.
8. *Golden calf*, xxxii: *a.* Moses' delay in the mount; *b.* Israel murmurs; *c.* calf made by Aaron; *d.* return of Moses; *e.* breaking of tables; *f.* anger of Jehovah; *g.* plea of Moses.

9. *Glory of Jehovah appears to Moses, Ex.* xxxiii—xxxiv: *a.* in tent; *b.* in cleft of rock; *c.* Moses hews two tables of stone; *d.* ascends (5th time) the mount; *e.* numerous commands for Israel; *f.* face of Moses shines.

Literature:

Geikie, Hours, vol. ii. chaps. 9 and 10.
Blaikie, Manual, chap. 6, sec. 2.
Edersheim, Bible History, vol. ii. chaps. 10–13.
Humphrey, Sacred History, chap. 23.
Stanley, Jewish Church, Lec. 7.
Rawlinson, Moses his Life and Times.
Harper, Bible and Modern Discoveries, on *Site of Sinai.*
Boardman, The Ten Commandments. Phila., 1889.
Green, W. H., The Hebrew Feasts.
Feasts in Bib. Dicts. and Encycs.

§33. DOINGS AND LAWS GIVEN AT SINAI IN LEV. AND NUM. I—IX.

1. *Offerings, Lev.* i—x; *Num.* xvi: (1) Kinds: *a.* sin; *b.* burnt; *c.* meal; *d.* peace; *e.* guilt or trespass. (2) Significance: *a.* sin—expiatory; *b.* burnt—self-dedicatory; *c.* meal and (*d*) peace—thanksgiving; *e.* trespass—expiatory. Cf. Rom. iii. 25; I Cor. i. 30.
2. *Foods prohibited and permitted, Lev.* xi: (read only).
3. *Laws of purification, Lev.* xii—xxii; *Num.* v. xix.

4. *Sabbatical and jubilee years, Lev.* xxv: *a.* laws of work; *b.* laws of redemption; *c.* application to the stranger.
5. *Enumeration of Israel and order of encampment, Num.* i—iv: *a.* number of Levites; *b.* work of Levites; *c.* order of tribes in camp.
6. *Nazarite vow, Num.* vi: *a.* special prohibitions; *b.* special work; *c.* special significance; *d.* some of the greatest Nazarites in history.
7. *Dedication of the altar,* vii., viii: *a.* order of tribes followed; *b.* sum of offerings; *c.* cleansing of the Levites.
8. *First passover observance, Num.* ix: *a.* time; *b.* commands; *c.* accompaniments; *d.* trumpet commands.

Literature:

Edersheim, Bib. History, vol. ii. chaps. 14 and 15. *Feasts, Passover Offering* in Bib. Dicts. and Encycs.

§34. FROM SINAI TO THE ARNON—NUM. X. 11— XXI. 13.

1. *Time of departure and order of March.*
2. *First halts,* x. 11—xii: *a.* Taberah, or Kibrath-Hataavah; *b.* murmurings of Israel; *c.* fire from Jehovah; *d.* cry for flesh; *e.* seventy elders appointed; *f.* prophets in camp; *g.* surfeit of quails; *h.* plague therefrom; *i.* in Hazeroth; *j.* Aaron and Miriam against Moses; *k.* Miriam's leprosy.

3. *Wilderness of Paran,* xiii–xiv: *a.* twelve spies sent out; *b.* extent of their search; *c.* return and double report—what was the sin of the spies? *d.* murmur of Israel—will go back to Egypt; *e.* Jehovah will destroy Israel; *f.* plea of Moses; *g.* Israel's sentence—to wander forty years; *h.* their anger—set upon the Canaanites in vain.
4. *Korah and his host,* xvi: *a.* 250 princes against Moses and Aaron—jealous ambition; *b.* Moses' test of his mission; *c.* earth swallows the host of Dathan and Abiram; *d.* fire from Jehovah on 250 burners of strange incense —Korahites.
5. *Priesthood of Levites established,* xvii—xviii; *a.* test of the rods; *b.* budding of Aaron's; *c.* charge of offerings put in Aaron's hands; *d.* tithe of Israel to Levi; *e.* Levi to give of his tithe a tithe.
6. *Wilderness of Zin,* xx. 1–13: *a.* death of Miriam; *b.* people murmur for water; *c.* rock smitten; *d.* Moses and Aaron punished for disobedience.

Probably a blank of thirty-seven years between verses 13 and 14 of chap. xx.

7. *Kadesh and Mt. Hor,* xx. 14—xxi. 3: *a.* Edom's refusal to Israel's request; *b.* Aaron's death and successor; *c.* Canaanites destroyed by Israel.

i

8. *Hor to Arnon*, xxi. 4–15: *a.* Red Sea—Ezion Geber; *b.* east of Mt. Seir; *c.* fiery serpents; *d.* serpent of brass—use in New Testament; *e.* stations near Arnon; *f.* location of Arnon; *g.* Book of Wars of Jehovah.

Literature:

Geikie, Hours, vol. ii. chap. 11.
Blaikie, Manual, chap. 6, sec. 3 and 4.
Edersheim, Bible History, vol. ii. chaps. 16–21.
Stanley, Jewish Church, Lec. 8, 1.
Smith, Old Test. Hist., chap. 13.
Trumbull, Kadesh Barnea, N. Y., 1884.
Price, Ira M., Lost writings quoted and referred to in the Old Testament, Bibliotheca Sacra, April, 1889.

§35. CONQUESTS EAST OF THE JORDAN—NUM. XXI. 13—XXXVI. 13.

1. *Victory over Sihon, king of the Amorites*, xxi. 21–32: *a.* request of Sihon; *b.* Sihon's refusal and charge; *c.* Israel's victory; *d.* Heshbon; *e.* ancient poems in verses 27–30.
2. *Victory over Og, king of Bashan*, xxi. 33–35: *a.* country of Bashan; *b.* people; *c.* capital; *d.* Israel's victory.
3. *Story of Balaam*, xxii: (1). Bamoth Baal: *a.* seven altars; *b.* offerings; *c.* parable; *d.* analyze. (2). Pisgah: *a.* altars; *b.* offerings: *c.* parable; *d.* analyze. (3). Peor: *a.* altars;

b. offerings; *c.* parable; *d.* analyze. (4). Spirit of Jehovah upon him: *a.* prophetic vision of future events.

<small>NOTE—*a.* the advance in the thought of the four poems; *b.* character of Balaam as depicted in the Bible; *c.* explain this phenomenon.</small>

5. *Sin of Israel with Moab,* xxv: *a.* alliances with Baal Peor; *b.* plague on Israel; *c.* Eleazar's means of staying the same.
6. *Sum of Israel,* xxvi: *a.* 601,730 and 23,000 Levites, cf. with Num. i—iv.
7. *Inheritance of the daughters of Manasseh,* xxvii. xxxvi: *a.* among their brethren; *b.* general law of inheritance.
8. *Israel's vengeance on the Moabites and Midianites,* xxxi: *a.* number of soldiers; *b.* accompaniments; *c.* victory and slain—Balaam; *d.* booty—$146,730 in gold.
9. *Allotments to Reuben, Gad and half-tribe of Manasseh,* xxxii: *a.* requests of these three; *b.* conditions of granting their request; *c.* size and boundaries of east of the Jordan.
10. *Cities of Refuge,* xxxv: *a.* reason for such; *b.* their number; *c.* location; *d.* inhabitants; *e.* laws regulating their use.

Literature:

Geikie, Hours, vol. ii. chap. 12.
Blaikie, chap. 6, secs. 5 and 6.
Edersheim, Bible History, vol. iii. chaps. 1–3.

Stanley, Jewish Church, Lecs. 8 and 9.
Hurlbut, Man. Bib. Geog., pp. 47, 48.
Stanley, Sinai and Palestine, chaps. 7 and 8.
Merrill, East of the Jordan, N. Y., 1883.
Thomson, Land and Book, vol. iii. chaps. 12–18.
Tristram, Land of Moab, N. Y., 1873.
Porter, Giant Cities of Bashan, N. Y., 1873.
Schumacher, Across the Jordan, London, 1886.
Geikie, Old Test. Characters, on *Balaam*.
Hengstenberg on *Balaam*, in Com. on Daniel.
Wilberforce, Heroes of Hebrew History.
Each proper name in Bib. Dicts. and Encycs.

§36. FINAL REVIEW AND DEATH OF MOSES — DEUTERONOMY.

1. *Review of past forty years*, i—iii: *a.* wilderness and Kadesh; *b.* journey to Arnon and victory over Amorites; *c.* Og smitten, and Joshua made successor to Moses.
2. *Exhortations*, iv. 1–40.
3. *Cities of refuge east of Jordan*, iv. 41–43.
4. *The ten commandments, w. commentary thereon*, iv. 44—xxvi. 19: *a.* circumstances of delivery; *b.* ten commandments; *c.* commentary on them, v. 22 — xii. 3; *d.* laws of religion in general, xii. 4 — xvi. 17; *e.* laws regulating government, xvi. 18—xxi. 23; *f.* laws regulating private and social life, xxii—xxvi; *g.* cf. Ex. xxi–xxiii.

5. *The blessing and the curse*, xxvii—xxx: *a.* at Ebal and Gerizim.
6. *Law in the hands of the Levites*, xxxi: *a* to preserve; *b.* to read to the people once in seven years.
7. *Song of Moses*, xxxii: *a.* analyze it; *b.* its character; *c.* its purpose.
8. *Blessings upon twelve tribes*, xxxiii: *a.* description or prophecy? *b.* compare tribe for tribe with Gen. xlix; *c.* do these words accord with Israel's subsequent history?
9. *Moses' ascent to Pisgah and his death*, xxxiv: *a* view of the promised land; *b.* death; *c.* burial—where? *d.* successor; *e.* Israel's camp, where?

Literature:

Additional to §35.
Blaikie, Manual, chap. vi. secs. 7 and 8.
Edersheim, Bible History, vol. iii. chap. 4.
Deuteronomy in Smith Bib. Dict.
Pisgah " " "
" Tristram's Land of Moab.

SIXTH PERIOD.

CONQUEST. ENTRANCE INTO CANAAN TO THE JUDGES, B. C. 1451–1400.

§37. THE ENTRANCE INTO CANAAN—JOSH. I–IX.

1. *Canaan, size, boundary, contour:* see §§2 and 3.
2. *Inhabitants of Canaan:* a. in lowlands and highlands; b. religion; c. nationality; d. warlikeness.
3. *Joshua:* I. a. early life; b. spy; c. warrior; d. devoted to Jehovah; e. Ephraimite. II. a. word of Jehovah to Joshua; b. word of Joshua to people; c. role of the two and a half tribes in the conquest.
4. *Spies despatched to Jericho:* a. purpose; b. condition of people of Jericho; c. Rahab; d. success of the spies.
5. *Crossing,* iii–iv; Ps. cxiv: a. three days for sanctification; b. order of crossing; c. twelve stones carried out; d. time—10th day of first month.
6. *Encampment in Canaan,* v: a. Gilgal, Hos. iv. 15; Judg. iii. 19, 26; b. rite of circumcision renewed, cf. Gen. xvii. 10–14; c. passover observed; d. manna ceased, second day after passover; e. vision of Joshua.

7. *Destruction of Jericho*, vi; Ps. xliv. 1–3: *a.* order of compassing the city; *b.* time and result on seventh day; *c.* Rahab saved, Matt. i. 5; Heb. xi. 31; Jas. ii. 25; *d.* curse on rebuilder of Jericho, cf. 1 Kings xvi. 34.
8. *Overthrow of Ai*, vii—viii. 29: *a.* first attack repulsed; *b.* Achan's sin and punishment; *c.* casting lot — what was it? *d.* Ai destroyed.
9. *First altar of Israel in Canaan*, viii. 30–35: *a.* of unhewn stone; *b.* according to the law of Moses; *c.* burnt and peace offerings; *d.* in Ebal; *e.* laws all read.

Literature:

Geikie, Hours, vol. ii. chap. 13.
Blaikie, Manual, chap. 7, secs. 1 and 2
Edersheim, Bible History, vol. iii. chaps. 5–8.
Stanley, Jewish Church, Lec. 10.
Hurlbut, Man. Bib. Geog., pp. 51–54.
Smith, Old Test. History, chap. 16.
Thomson, Land and Book, vol. iii.
Deane, B., Joshua, his Life and Times—Men of the Bible Series.
Geikie, Old Test. Characters, on *Joshua*.
Joshua in Bible Dict. and Encycs.

§38. THE SOUTHERN CAMPAIGN—JOSHUA IX—X.

1. *Terror among the nations*, ix. 1, 2.
2. *Gibeon's deceit and success*, ix. 3–27: *a.* ambassador from far-off country—mention only

wars east of Jordan; *b.* Joshua's compassion and treaty; *c.* consequences to Gibeon; *d.* results to Israel—(cf. 2 Sam. xxi. 1–11).

3. *Conspiracy against Gibeon,* x. 1–5: *a.* five kings combine; *b.* besiege the fortress of Gibeon.
4. *Great battle at Gibeon,* x. 6–14: *a.* Gibeonites call to Joshua; *b.* Israel's night march; *c.* onset at daybreak with the shout, "God is mighty in battle, God is his name;" *d.* defeat and pursuit to Beth-horon; *e.* hailstones (cf. Judg. iv. 15 and v. 21; 1 Sam. vii. 10) and victory.
5. *Joshua's prayer,* x. 12, 13: *a.* sun standing still —explanations (cf. Stanley, p. 221 sq.; Josephus v. 1, §4); *b.* book of Jashar (cf. 2 Sam. i. 18–27); *c.* consider that (1) it is poetry (cf. Judg. v. 20; Ps. xcviii. 8; xcvii. 5; Isa. lv. 12), (2) it is a quotation, (3) the doctrine of inspiration demands only that we have an accurate text of the passage quoted, cf. also Geikie, vol. ii. p. 417.
6. *Slaughter of the five kings,* x. 16–27: *a.* hidden and caught in a cave; *b.* brought forth and trodden upon; *c.* slain and hanged till evening (cf. Deut. xxi. 23); *d.* buried in the cave.
8. *Further conquests,* x. 28–43: *a.* Makkedah; *b.* Libnah; *c.* Lachish; *d.* Eglon; *e.* Hebron; *f.* South Country; *g.* Kadesh Barnea to Gaza; *i.* return to Gilgal.

8. *Cities and kings destroyed*, xii. 9-18.

Literature:

Additional to §37.
Edersheim, Bible History, vol. iii. chaps. 9 and 10.
Stanley, Jewish Church, Lec. 11.
Price, Lost Writings, etc., Bib. Sacra, April '89, on *Book of Jashar*.

§39. THE NORTHERN CAMPAIGN—JOSH. XI.

1. *The Northern combination*, xi. 1-5: *a.* leader; *b.* composition of the army; *c.* camp, where? *d.* first mention of Merom; *e.* peoples and lands represented.
2. *Jehovah's command and assurance to Joshua*, xi. 6.
3. *Israel's attack and victory*, xi. 7-15: *a.* sudden attack; *b.* surprise and rout of the enemy; *c.* destruction of horses (first use mentioned) and chariots; *d.* cities and spoil saved, except Hazor, but people all destroyed.
4. *Summary of Joshua's conquests*, xi. 16-23: *a.* all he met he destroyed, except the Gibeonites; *b.* it was of Jehovah; *c.* Anakim, near Hebron, destroyed.
5. *Summary of kings slain*, xii. 19-24.
6. *The extermination of the Canaanites:* *a.* **Canaan** belonged to Jehovah to do as he chose therewith; *b.* providential history proceeds with seeming indifference to life—floods, pestilence,

famine, etc.; *c.* it was in accordance with an explicit command of Jehovah (cf. Deut. vii. 1–5) that they should have been destroyed; *d.* Arnold, in Sermons vi. 35–37 says: "The Israelites' sword, in its bloodiest executions, wrought a work of mercy to all the countries of the earth to the very end of the world."

Literature:

Addional to §§37 and 38.

Stanley, Jewish Church, Lec. 12.

On *Extermination of the Canaanites* consult the following:

Northrup, Dr. G. W., "The Standard," April 21, 1881.

Stanley, Jewish Church, Lec. 11, pp. 223-8.

Hengstenberg, Genuineness of the Pentateuch, vol. ii. pp. 387–417.

North American Review, 1882.

Oehler, Old Testament Theology (Day's Trans.), pp. 81-85.

Mozley, Lectures on Old Testament, Lec. 4.

§40. SETTLEMENT OF THE TRIBES—JOSH. XIII—XXII.

1. *East of the Jordan*, xiii; Num. xxxii. 1-38: *a.* Reuben; *b.* Gad; *c.* half-tribe of Manasseh.
2. *Levites and Caleb*, xiv., xxi: *a.* Levites in cities —48 and suburbs; *b.* in cities of refuge (See §35, 10); *c.* distribution and number west of Jordan; *d.* Caleb's inheritance.

3. *Judah*, xv: *a.* boundaries; *b.* number of cities possessed; *c.* character of territory; *d.* chief city—Hebron.
4. *Ephraim*, xvi: *a.* location and boundaries; *b.* contour of country; *c.* chief cities—Shiloh and Shechem.
5. *Manasseh*, xvii: *a.* adjacent to Ephraim; *b.* boundaries; *c.* chief city—Samaria.
6. *Tent of meeting located,* (xviii. 1–10) *and twenty one surveyors sent out:* *a.* Shiloh, religious headquarters; *b.* seven tribes to be provided for.
7. *Benjamin*, xviii. 11–28: *a.* boundaries; *b.* cities by number; *c.* chief city—Jerusalem.
8. *Simeon*, xix. 1–9: *a.* boundaries; *b.* number of cities.
9. *Zebulon*, xix. 10–16: *a.* boundaries—no water-lines; *b.* number of cities.
10. *Issachar*, xix. 17–23: *a.* location; *b.* boundary; *c.* cities.
11. *Asher*, xix. 24–31: *a.* amount of sea coast; *b.* boundary to east; *c.* cities.
12. *Naphtali*, xix. 32–39: *a.* sources of Jordan; *b.* bound otherwise; *c.* cities and villages.
13. *Dan*, xix. 40–48: *a.* exact boundaries; *b.* size; *c.* character of the country.
14. *Departure of East-Jordanic tribes*, xxii: *a.* Joshua's charge; *b.* altar built at Jordan; *c.* suspicions and wrath of West-Jordanic tribes; *d.* interview results in peace.

15. *Draw a tribal map of Palestine, indicating for each tribe:* *a.* boundaries; *b.* chief cities; *c.* principal mountain points.

Literature:

Geikie, Hours, vol. ii. latter part of chap. 13.
Blaikie, Manual, chap. 7, sec. 3.
Edersheim, Bible History, vol. iii. chaps. 11 and 12.
Stanley, Jewish Church, Lec. 12.
Hurlbut, Man. of Bib. Geog., pp. 55–59.
Osborn's Map of Palestine.
Joshua, His Life and Times, Men of Bible Series.

§41. JOSHUA'S DEPARTURE AND CONDITION OF THE LAND.—JOSHUA XXIII—XXIV.

1. *Joshua's parting words,* xxiii: *a.* allotment of nations to Israel; *b.* observe the law of Moses; *c.* courage and victory consequent on obedience; *d.* alliance with these peoples is destruction; *e.* God's promises to *me* are fulfilled; *f.* if *you* forsake God, destruction will follow.
2. *Joshua's historic review and covenant,* xxiv. 2–28: *a.* outline history from Abraham to present; *b.* call to put away other gods; *c.* people resolve to serve Jehovah; *d.* Joshua's denial and covenant; *e.* stone set up as a witness.
3. *Joshua's death,* xxiv. 29–30; Judg ii. 6–10: *a.* 110 years old; *b.* buried in Timnath-Serah in Ephraim.

4. *Burial of Joseph's bones*, xxiv. 32: *a.* brought from Egypt; *b.* buried in Shechem; *c.* other sacred associations at Shechem.
5. *Tribes all settled:* *a.* east of Jordan—which ones? *b.* west of Jordan—which? *c.* location of each tribe.
6. *Remains of unconquered peoples*, Judg. i: *a.* fortresses—in which tribes? *b.* towns; *c.* migrations— according to tradition.
7. *Some results of the conquest:* *a.* settlement of Israel as a nation; *b.* living and constant contact with the Canaanites; *c.* establishment of laws of inheritance, etc., cf. Boaz, Ruth, Barzillai and Naboth.

Literature:

Additional to §40 :

Blaikie, Manual, chap. 7, sec. 4.

Edersheim, Bible History, vol. iii. chap. 12.

Geikie, Old Test. Characters, on *Joshua*.

§42. SUPPLEMENTARY TO THE CONQUEST.—JUDG. I., XVII—XXI.

1. *Conquests of Judah, Simeon and Joseph*, i: *a.* against Adoni-bezek; *b.* Jerusalem; *c.* Canaanites; *d.* Bethel.
2. *Danite migration*, xvii., xviii: *a.* Micah; *b.* kind of idolatry rife; *c.* the Levite; *d.* his employer; *e.* Danite spies; *f.* result of their trip; *g.* advance of the army and robbery of Micah; *h.* new territory acquired, and its boundaries—Laish, Dan.

3. *Civil war*, xix—xxi: *a.* cause (cf. 1 Sam. xi. 7), revealing corruptness of Israel; *b.* national indignation; *c.* assembly at Mizpeh; *d.* 400,000 men against Benjamin; *e.* repulses of Israel; *f.* defeat of Benjamin and reduction to 600; *g.* means of finding wives for these.
4. *Israel's tendency to idolatry in Judges due to:* *a.* ease in quiet homes; *b.* language common with the Canaanites; *c.* intermarriage with Canaanites; *d.* want of a leader—no central power; *e.* lack of defenses—no army organization.
5. *Ancient seats of worship:* *a.* Mt. Carmel; *b.* Mt. Tabor; *c.* Baal-gad; *d.* Bethel.
6. *Seats of worship at this time* (cf. Zech. x. 2; Hos. iii. 4; 2 Kings xxiii. 24; 1 Sam. xix. 16): *a.* in every home; *b.* with teraphim, etc.; *c.* attended by a priest; *d.* in imitation of the Canaanites.

Literature:

Blaikie, Manual, chap. 8, secs. 2 and 3.
Edersheim, Bible History, vol. iii. chaps. 13 and 21.
Stanley, Jewish Church, Lec. 13, secs. 1, 4–6.
Hurlbut, Man. Bib. Geog., p. 61.

SEVENTH PERIOD.

JUDGES. RULE OF JUDGES TO ESTABLISHMENT OF KINGDOM. B. C. 1400—1095.

SEVEN OPPRESSIONS AND FIFTEEN JUDGES.

§43. FIRST THREE OPPRESSIONS AND THREE JUDGES.—JUDGES II. 11—III. 31.

1. *Introduction to this Period*, ii. 11—iii. 6: *a.* Israel did evil—served other gods; *b.* anger of Jehovah against Israel; *c.* purpose of Jehovah in leaving unconquered peoples in the land, iii. 1–6.
2. *Mesopotamian invasion*, iii. 7–11: *a.* home of oppressors; *b.* king of oppressors; *c.* length of time of oppression; *d.* deliverers; *e.* peace for 40 years.

    Othniel, first judge, of Judah.
3. *Moabite oppression*, iii. 12–30: *a.* Moab, with Ammon and Amalek, smite Israel and take Jericho; *b.* separate homes of these peoples; *c.* king of Moab; *d.* years of oppression; *e.* Ehud, of Benjamin, slew Eglon; *f.* slaughter at Jordan—how great? *g.* land had rest 80 years.

1

Ehud, second judge, of Benjamin.
4. *First Philistine oppression,* iii. 31.
Shamgar, third judge, deliverer.

Review: Give of the three oppressions: *a.* oppressor; *b.* length of oppression; *c.* deliverers; *d.* time of rest.

Literature:

Geikie, Hours, vol. ii. chap. 14 and part of 15.
Blaikie, Manual, chap. 8, sec. 1.
Edersheim, Bible History, vol. iii. chap. 14.
Stanley, Jewish Church, Lec. 14 in part.
Hurlbut, Man. Bib. Geog., pp. 61, 62.
Smith, Old Test. History, chap. 8.
Expositor's Bible, Judges and Ruth.

§44. CANAANITE AND MIDIANITE OPPRESSIONS.—
JUDGES IV—VIII.

1. *Canaanite oppression,* iv: *a.* oppressors — natives of the land; *b.* 20 years oppression; *c.* army of 900 chariots of iron; *d.* Deborah, of Ephraim, arouses Barak, of Naphtali; *e.* Issachar, Zebulon and Naphtali at Tabor meet and rout the host of Sisera; *f.* storm aids; *g.* Jael's murder of Sisera; *h.* "God subdued Jabin, the king of Canaan;" *i.* land had rest 40 years; *j.* similar battles in history, (1) Cressy, (2) Timoleon against the Carthaginians.

Deborah, fourth judge, of Ephraim.

2. *Deborah's song*, v: analyze, noting *a*. the prelude; *b*. reference to exodus; *c*. dismay of Israel; *d*. change; *e*. assembling of troops; *f*. recreants who did not appear; *g*. battle and flight; *h*. destroyer; *i*. mother in anxiety; *j*. the triumph.

3. *Midianite oppression*, vi—viii: *a*. Amalek, Midian and children of the East oppress Israel *seven* years; *b*. Israel's abject cowardice: (1) hidden in rocks, (2) caves, (3) strongholds; *c*. a prophet appears; *d*. Gideon's call: (1) the angel, (2) offering of Gideon, (3) altar built; *e*. destruction of Baal worship; *f*. evidence of truth of God's word—fleece; *g*. army called: (1) faint-hearted return, (2) lappers only remain—300; *h*. dream of the Midianite; *i*. victory of 300; *j*. results: (1) attempt to establish a royal line, (2) teraphim made of the spoils—Gideon its priest, (3) Gideon polygamous, (4) leads Israel astray, (5) land had rest 40 years.

Gideon, fifth judge, of Manasseh.

4. *Abimelech*, ix: *a*. son of a maid of Shechem; *b*. appears to Shechemites for his claim; *c*. is granted a subsidy; *d*. slays seventy brethren, except Jotham; *e*. Jotham's parable, first in history (olive, fig, vine, bramble); *f*. **Abimelech made king in Shechem;** *g*. rules

three years; *h.* fights three battles—Shechem assaulted; *i.* slain by a millstone dropped by a woman at Thebez.

Abimelech, sixth judge, of Manasseh.

Review: Give *a.* location of the oppressors; *b.* time; *c.* severity of the oppression; *d.* deliverer in each case.

Judges thus far: 1. Othniel; 2. Ehud; 3. Shamgar; 4. Deborah (and Barak); 5. Gideon; 6. Abimelech.

Literature:

Geikie, Hours, vol. ii. chaps. 15 and 16 in part.
Blaikie, Manual, chap. 8, sec. 1.
Edersheim, Bible History, vol. iii. chaps. 15–17.
Stanley, Jewish Church, Lec. 14 in part and 15.
Hurlbut, Man. Bib. Geog., p. 62.
Thomson, Land and Book, vol. ii. p. 179 sq.
Geikie, Old Test. Characters, on *Jael, Deborah, Gideon.*
Mozley, Lectures on the Old Testament, Lecs. 6 and 7.
Expositor's Bible, Judges and Ruth.

§45. AMMONITE AND PHILISTINE OPPRESSIONS.— JUDGES X—XI.

1. *Tola, seventh judge, of Issachar,* x. 1, 2: *a.* abode in Shamir of Ephraim; *b.* judged Israel 23 years.

2. *Jair, eighth judge, Gileadite*, x. 3–5: *a.* had 30 sons who rode 30 ass-colts; *b.* had 30 cities; *c.* judged Israel 22 years.
3. *Ammonite oppression*, x. 6—xii. 7: *a.* Israel's idolatry; *b.* oppression 18 years; *c.* distress of Israel; *d.* Jehovah's message and Israel's resolve at Mizpeh; *e.* Jephthah chosen as leader; *f.* his conditional acceptance; *g.* message to Ammon and reply; *h.* Jephthah's vow; *i.* slaughter—20 cities; *j.* reception at home; *k.* daughter's valor and lament; *l.* vow performed (cf. §24. 8); *m.* memorial four days in the year; *n.* Jephthah's slaughter of the jealous Ephraimites—Shibboleth test. *Jephthah, ninth* judge, six years.
4. *Compare the characters of Gideon and Jephthah.*
5. *Ibzan, tenth judge, of Bethlehem*, xii. 8–10: *a.* had 30 sons and 30 daughters; *b.* judged Israel seven years.
6. *Elon, eleventh judge, of Zebulon*, x. 11, 12: judged Israel ten years.
7. *Abdon, twelfth judge, of Ephraim*, xii. 13–15: *a.* had 40 sons and 30 grandsons, who rode on 70 asses; *b.* judged Israel eight years.
8. *Samson, of Dan, and the Philistine oppression*, (40 years), xiii—xvi: *a.* appeal of Manoah; *b.* angel of Jehovah; *c.* birth of Samson; *d.* spirit of Jehovah upon him; *e.* finds a woman in Timnath; *f.* kills a lion; *g.* wedding-

feast; *h.* riddle; *i.* solution, and slaughter of the Ashkelonites; *j.* wife given away and grain burnt by 300 jackals; *k.* hides in Etam; *l.* Israel delivers him up—slays 1000 Philistines with the jaw-bone of an ass; *m.* carries off gates of Gaza; *n.* Delilah's treachery, Samson's humility; *o.* final Philistine clown and destroyer; *p.* judged Israel 20 years.

Samson, thirteenth judge, of Dan.

NOTE—*Samson* the first recorded Nazarite.

Literature:

Geikie, Hours, vol. ii. chap. 16; vol. iii. chap. 1.
Edersheim, Bible History, vol. iii. chaps. 18–20.
Stanley, Jewish Church, Lec. 16.
Smith, Old Test. History, chaps. 18 and 19.
Hurlbut, Man. Bib. Geog., pp. 63, 64.
Geikie, Old Test. Characters, on *Jephthah, Samson and Delilah.*
Expositor's Bible, Judges and Ruth.

§46. RUTH.—RUTH I—IV.

1. *Time:* *a.* when judges judged; *b.* famine in land *c.* mention other famines already met in our study.
2. *Emigration to Moab:* *a.* names of persons; *b.* alliances made there; *c.* fatalities.
3. *Return to Israel:* *a.* report of plenty; *b.* Naomi's company and request; *c.* Orpah obeys,

Ruth clings to her mother-in-law; *d.* arrival at Bethlehem.
4. *Court transactions:* *a.* Ruth gleans in Boaz's field; *b.* received with favor; *c.* promise of Boaz; *d.* redemption council; *e.* nearest kinsman failing, Boaz redeems; *f.* attestation by an old shoe; *g.* Ruth becomes wife of Boaz.
5. *Purpose of the book:* *a.* give us a charming domestic incident in the midst of the dark ages of the judges; *b.* beautiful and vivid picture of one of the ancestors of our Lord (iv. 18–22).
6. *Compare this book with Esther.*

Literature:

Blaikie, Manual, chap. 8, sec. 3 (4).
Edersheim, Bible History, vol. iii. chap. 21.
Geikie, Old Testament Characters, on *Ruth*.
Expositor's Bible, Judges and Ruth.
Ruth, in Bib. Dicts. and Encycs.

§47. ELI AND THE FALL OF SHILOH.—I SAM. I. 7—II.

1. *First appearance of Eli,* i. 9, 14–17: *a.* priest at door of temple of Jehovah; *b.* rebuking Hannah; *c.* favorable answer to Hannah.
2. *Sons of Eli,* ii. 12–17, 22–25: *a.* sons of Belial, (1) in priest's office, (2) in private life; *b.* Eli's mild rebuke; *c.* Eli's sin (vs. 29).
3. *Message of Man of God,* ii. 27–36: *a.* God's

past goodness disregarded; *b.* certain downfall of Eli's house; *c.* a faithful priest to rise up; *d.* sure house and faithful service forever (cf. xvi. 13; 1 Chron.xvii.13;Ps. xcix. 6).
4. *Visions of Samuel for Eli*, iii. 11–18: *a.* curse on Eli's house because of his lack of restraint of his sons; *b.* curse not to be purged by sacrifice; *c.* Eli's submission.
5. *Loss of the ark and Eli's death*, iv. 1–18: *a.* Israel loses 4,000 men in the first battle with the Philistines; *b.* Philistines capture the ark in second battle and slay Eli's sons; *c.* Philistines supposed they had captured Jehovah (cf. Hosea x. 6; Isa. xlvi. 1; Jer. xlviii. 7; xlix. 3; Dan. xi. 8); *d.* sad news breaks Eli's heart and neck; *e.* 98 years old; *f.* judge 40 years.

Eli, fourteenth judge, a Levite.

6. *Shiloh:* *a.* what became of the tabernacle (cf. 2 Chron. i. 5; v. 5)? *b.* where did Samuel go? *c.* was Shiloh laid waste by the Philistines (Ps. lxxviii. 60, 67; Jer. vii. 12, 14; cf. 1 Kings xi. 29)?
7. *The ark in Philistia and returned*, v. 1—vii. 2: *a.* at Ashdod, (1) Dagon humbled, (2) plague of tumors, (3) ark sent to Gath; *b.* at Gath, (2) city smitten, (2) tumors on all; *c.* at Ekron, (1) plague follows, (2) priests advise return with a guilt offering; *d.* returned to Beth-shemesh, (1) cart and cows, (2) go

straight ahead; *e.* fatality in Beth-shemesh; *f.* ark in Kirjath-jearim twenty years.

Literature:

Geikie, Hours, vol. iii. chaps. 1 in part and 2.
Blaikie, Manual, pp. 205–6.
Edersheim, Bible History, vol. iv. chaps. 1–3.
Stanley, Jewish Church, Lec. 17.
O. T. Student, Sept. 1887, pp. 27–30.
Geikie, Old Test. Characters, on *Eli*.
Expositor's Bible, First Samuel.

§48. SAMUEL AS JUDGE AND RULER TO ACCESSION OF SAUL.—I SAM. I—XI.

1. *Hannah's victory*, i: *a.* request; *b.* promise; *c.* son—Nazarite (cf. §33, 6); *d.* consecration at Shiloh.
2. *Hannah's prayer*, ii. (cf. Anna, in Tobit. i. 9; Luke ii. 36): *a.* analyze it; *b.* similar song Luke i. 46–55, 67–79; *c.* first individual (*not* national) song.
3. *Samuel's ministry with Eli*, iii. 1—iv. 1: *a.* thrice called; *b.* God's curse on Eli; *c.* Samuel established as a prophet; *d.* revelations to him for Israel.
4. *After twenty years' silence, Samuel is judge*, vii. 3–14: *a.* host at Mizpeh turn to Jehovah (pour out water, cf. Josh. vii. 5; Ps. xxii. 14; Lam. ii. 19); *b.* Samuel cries to Jehovah against the Philistines; *c.* Jehovah thundered

against the Philistines with a mighty storm; *d.* Eben-ezer set up.

5. *Samuel is circuit judge,* vii. 15—viii. 22: *a.* altar and home in Ramah; *b.* annual circuit, Bethel, Gilgal, and Mizpeh; *c.* his sons pervert judgment in Beer-sheba; *d.* demand of the people for a king; *e.* Jehovah's answer to Samuel; *f.* second demand and Jehovah's command that Samuel make them a king.
6. *Samuel's earlier relations to Saul,* ix. 1—xi. 13: *a.* Saul and the lost asses; *b.* Samuel anoints Saul king; *c.* Samuel assembles the people at Mizpeh, and Saul chosen by lot; *d.* Samuel's part in the Ammonite war.

Literature:

Geikie, Hours, vol. iii. chap. 3.
Edersheim, Bible History, vol. iv. chaps. 1-3 in part, all of 4-6.
Stanley, Jewish Church, Lecs. 18 and 19.
Samuel and Saul, Men of Bible Series.
Edersheim, Prophecy and History in relation to the Messiah, Lec. 2.
Briggs, Messianic Prophecy, chap. 5, §40.
Expositor's Bible, First Samuel.

§49. SAMUEL UNDER A KING, SAUL.—I SAM. XII., XIII. 8-15; XV., XVI. 1-13; XIX. 18-22.

1. *Samuel's address,* xii: *a.* Saul made king in Gilgal; *b.* Samuel retires because (1) Israel has a king, (2) he is old; *c.* challenge to im-

peach his past honesty; *d.* epitome of past mercies upon penitent idolaters; *e.* king set up at people's request; *f.* favor of God dependent on obedience; *g.* thunder of God's anger against sin; *h.* Samuel's prayer without ceasing.

2. *Samuel's rebuke of Saul*, xiii. 8–15: *a.* at Gilgal in presence of Philistine army; *b. first* prophecy of downfall of his kingdom; *c.* command to smite Amalek; *d.* disobedience condemned; *e.* Saul's penitence unrewarded, downfall of his kingdom prophesied second time.

3. *Samuel anoints a second king, David, over Israel* —xvi. 1–13: *a.* Jehovah rejects Saul; *b.* Samuel visits Jesse at Bethlehem to sacrifice; *c.* of eight sons, Jehovah chooses the youngest, David; *d.* Samuel anoints him successor to Saul; *e.* spirit of Jehovah on David; *f.* Samuel goes to Ramah.

4. *Samuel in Ramah*, xix. 18–22: *a.* his home, altar and place of worship (vii.17): *b.* Samuel head of the school of prophets (xix. 20); *c.* Ramah prophetic headquarters; *d.* David escapes to Samuel; *e.* Saul likewise falls in with same spirit of prophesying; *f.* Samuel died in Ramah (xxv. 1) mourned for by all Israel.

5. *Character of the period:* *a.* end of the theocracy, beginning of the monarchy; *b.* blend-

ing of worship in Shiloh with new order of priests; *c.* beginning of the order of prophets —schools; *d.* water-shed between darkness and light; *e.* water-shed between oppression and peace.

6. *Character of Samuel and his place in history:* *a.* a Levite, his grandson was Heman the singer, 1 Chron. vi. 28, 33; *b.* a writer, 1 Sam. x. 25; 1 Chron. xxix. 29; *c.* judge; *d.* priest; *e.* prophet; *f.* anointed Saul and David; *g.* established schools of prophets; *h.* influence recognized in later times, cf. 1 Chron. xi. 3; ix. 22; xxvi. 28; *i.* compare him with Moses, Jer. xv. 1; Ps. xcix. 6; 2 Chron. xxxv. 18.

7. *Samuel's appearance to the witch of Endor,* xxviii. 3–25.

8. *Locate the geographical points of this section:* *a.* Gilgal; *b.* Bethlehem; *c.* Ramah; *d.* Mizpeh; *e.* Endor.

Literature:

Geikie, Hours, vol. iii. chap. 4 (pp. 40–92).
Blaikie, Manual, chap. 9, sec. 1.
Edersheim, Bible History, vol. iv. chaps. 7–9.
Stanley, Jewish Church, Lecs. 18 and 19.
Smith, Old Test. History, chap. 19.
Samuel and Saul, Men of Bible Series.
Blaikie, Expositor's Bible, First Samuel.
Price, Ira M., Schools of the Sons of the Prophets, Old Test. Student, March '89.
Magic, in Smith's Bible Dictionary.
Geikie, O. T. Characters, on *Samuel.*

EIGHTH PERIOD.

THE KINGDOM. ESTABLISHMENT TO DISRUPTION. B. C. 1095-975.

---

§50. SAUL'S SANE CAREER—I SAM. IX—XVIII..

1. *Discovery, anointing and election*, ix–x.26: *a.* man of God—Samuel; *b.* events of the feast; *c.* Saul anointed; *d.* Saul among prophets (cf. xix. 18–24); *e.* elected by lot—what was the lot?
2. *Ammonite war*, xi: *a.* location and territory of Ammonites; *b.* ancestry; *c.* call of East-Jordanic peoples for help; *d.* Saul's response and victory; *e.* confirmed as king of Israel.
3. *First Philistine invasion*, xiii: *a.* Israel 3,000 men; *b.* Philistine outposts; *c.* Jonathan's victory over outpost at Geba; *d.* Philistine army 30,000 chariots, 6,000 horsemen, people as sand on the sea—encamped at Michmash; *e.* Israel's flight to Gilgal; *f.* Saul's sacrilege; *g.* Samuel's rebuke and prophecy; *h.* Philistine guerillas—three bands; *i.* Israel without arms.
4. *Saul's victory*, xiv. 1–46: *a.* Jonathan's strategy and success; *b.* general flight of Philistines; *c.* Saul's vow—cause of it; *d.* Jonathan the

i

only violator; *c.* Saul's first altar, and sacrifice by the people; *f.* Jonathan saved from death by the people.

5. *Saul's minor wars*, xiv. 47–48: I. *a.* Moab, cf. Gen. xix. 37; *b.* Ammon, Gen.xix. 38, cf. chap. xi; *c.* Edom, cf. xxi. 7; xxii. 9, 18; *d.* Zobah.—extreme north; *e.* Philistines. II. *a.* location; *b.* ancestry; *c.* character of people; *d.* relations to Israel of each of the above-mentioned peoples.

6. *Amalekite war*, xv: *a.* wholesale slaughter commanded—why? *b.* not executed; *c.* Saul's equivocal reply to Samuel; *d.* Samuel's announcement of a great truth (xxii. 23); *e.* second prophecy of end of Saul's kingdom; *f.* Saul's penitence unrewarded; *g.* Samuel hews Agag to pieces.

7. *Second Philistine war*, xvii–xviii. 5: *a.* location; *b.* Israel defied forty days; *c.* David's deliverance of Israel; *d.* reward given—court favors; *e.* covenant of David and Jonathan.

Literature:

Hurlbut, Man. of Bib. Geog., pp. 65, 66.
Geikie, Hours, vol. iii. chap. 4.
Blaikie, Manual, chap. 9, sec. 1.
Edersheim, Bible History, vol. iv. chaps. 7–10.
Stanley, Jewish Church, Lec. 21.
Smith, O. T. History, chap. 20 in part.
Samuel and Saul, Men of Bible Series.

Blaikie, Expositor's Bible, First Samuel.
O. T. Student, Oct. 1887, pp. 53-57.
Oehler, O. T. Theology, §§164, 194.
Delitzsch, History of Redemption, p. 84 sq.
Geikie, Old Testament Characters, on *Saul*.

§51. SAUL'S INSANE CAREER.—XVI. 14-23; XVIII. 6—XXVI. 25, 28, 31.

1. *Evil spirit upon Saul*, xvi. 14-23: *a*. musician David sought out; *b*. David made his armourbearer; harmonize xvi. 14-23 with §50.7.
2. *Saul's jealousy*, xviii. 6—xix. 10: *a*. at David's popularity; *b*. Saul attempts to entrap and kill David, (*1*) by his spear—twice, (*2*) by his daughters, (*3*) by the Philistines.
3. *Saul's first pursuit of David*, xix. 11-24: *a*. messenger deceived by Michal; *b*. David's flight to Ramah to Samuel; *c*. Saul's three sets of messengers sent to take David, prophesy; *d*. Saul's attempt to capture David, results in his prophesying.

NOTE—Naioth—buildings, college buildings?

4. *Saul's second pursuit of David*, xx-xxiv: *a*. Jonathan's test of Saul's purpose toward David; *b*. feast and Saul's anger at Jonathan; *c*. arrows, and parting of Jonathan and David; *d*. David's flight and hiding places: (*1*) Nob: (*a*) shew-bread, (*b*) sword of Goliath, (*c*) Doeg, the Edomite of Saul's guard; (*2*)

Gath: (*a*) Fear of Phil., (*b*) madness feigned; (*3*) cave of Adullam: (*a*) his family there, (*b*) 400 men there; (*4*) Mizpeh of Moab, (*a*) prophet Gad appears, (*b*) David in the hold; (*5*) forest of Hereth, Saul at home has priests slain by Doeg the Edomite; (*6*) Keilah, David routs the Philistines in battle; (*7*) Ziph; (*8*) Maon, Saul surrounds David but a Philistine raid calls him home; (*9*) Engedi: (*a*) Saul in David's hands, but spared, (*b*) Saul's penitence and forgiveness, (*c*) Saul returns in peace.

5. *Saul's third pursuit of David*, xxvi: *a*. hill of Hachilah; *b*. David takes Saul's cruse and spear; *c*. Saul forgives David, and returns never again to see him.

6. *Saul's inquiries of the witch of. Endor*, xxviii: *a*. Philistines pitched in Shunem, Israel in Gilboa; *b*. Saul's former treatment of witches (vss. 3, 9); *c*. Jehovah answered him not by dreams, Urim or prophets; *d*. appeal to the witch of Endor; *e*. Samuel, *not at the call of the witch*, appears; *f*. prophecy of Israel's defeat; *g*. Saul's humility; *h*. explain "to-morrow shalt thou and thy sons be with me."

7. *Saul's death on Gilboa*, xxxi: *a*. suicide in defeat; *b*. body and armor distributed in Philistia; *c*. people of Jabesh burn and bury Saul's and his sons' bones.

8. *Character of the period:* a. religious condition of the times, cf. xvi. 1–6; xix. 18–24; xix. 13; xv., xxiii., xx. 18, 24–29; xxi. 1–9; xxii. 6–19; b. political condition, cf. xi., xiii., xiv., xv., xxxi.
9. *Character of Saul:* a. religious, xiv. 18, 19; xiv. 24, cf. with xiv. 31–35; xiv. 36–44.
   - (*1*) not converted—had simply a religious impulse.
   - (*2*) opposition to prophets, cf. xv., xxviii. 6.
   - (*3*) names of his sons: Jonathan=gift of Jehovah; Melchi-shua=help of Moloch; Merib-baal=strife of Baal.
   - (*4*) superstitious.
   - (*5*) jealousy, insane-madness.
10. *Follow carefully and locate David's hiding-places in his flights before Saul.* Give events at each point; cf. Hurlbut, Man. of Bib. Geog. pp. 66, 67.

Literature:

Same as §50 and additional thereto:
Geikie, Hours, vol. iii., chap. 5.
Edersheim, Bible History, vol. iv., chaps. 11–14.
Hurlbut, Man. Bib. Geog. pp. 66, 67.

§52. DAVID'S PRE-REGAL CAREER.—I SAM. XVI–XXX; I CHRON. XI. 10—XII. 20.

1. *Prophecies concerning David:* a. 1 Sam. xiii. 14; b. 1 Sam. xv. 28.

1

2. *Discovery, anointing and favor of David*, xvi: See §49. 3.
3. *David's victory over Goliath*, xvii. 12–58: *a.* method of fighting; *b.* result (*1*) to Israel, (*2*) to David himself. See §50. 7.
4. *Saul's jealousy*, xviii. 6—xix. 10: See §51. 2.
5. *David's first flight before Saul*, xix. 11–24. See §51. 3.

   NOTE.—(1) Saul's attempted capture of David produces prophets, (2) Saul himself becomes a prophet.

6. *David's second flight before Saul*, xx–xxiv: See §51. 4.
7. *David's treatment of Nabal*, xxv: *a.* David's request, why made? *b.* refused and trouble averted only by Abigail; *c.* death of Nabal and disposal of Abigail.
8. *David's third flight before Saul*, xxvi: See §51. 5.
9. *David's sojourn in Philistia*, xxvii–xxviii. 2: *a* in favor with king Achish; *b.* given Ziklag, his army here, 1 Chron. xii. 1–7; *c.* David raided country toward the southwest, destroying all; *d.* deceived Achish.
10. *David in the Philistine army against Israel*, xxix-–xxx: *a.* David and his men follow in rear; *b.* princes object and David returns; *c.* finds Ziklag destroyed — by whom? *d.* recovers captives; *e.* division of spoil among his benefactors.

11. *Locate every geographical point here mentioned.*
12. *Probable Psalms of this period*: *a.* of shepherd life, Pss. viii. xxi. xxiii. xxix; *b.* flight from Saul, vi. vii. lix. lvi. xxxiv; *c.* wanderings, xviii. xl. lii. liv. lvii. lxiii. cxlii.

Literature:

Geikie, Hours, vol. iii. chaps. 6 and 7.
Blaikie, Manual, chap. 9. sec. 2.
Edersheim, Bible History, vol. iv. chaps. 10–14.
Stanley, Jewish Church, Lec. 22.
Hurlbut, Man. Bib. Geog., pp. 66, 67.
Smith, Old Test. History, chap. 20.
Old Test. Student, Oct. 1887.
Edersheim, Prophecy and History in Relation to the Messiah, pp. 183–190.
Delitzsch, History of Redemption, pp. 84–94.
Geikie, Old Test. Characters, on *David the Shepherd, Goliath.*

§53. DAVID'S PROSPEROUS REIGN.—2 SAM. I—XI. 1; XII. 26–31; I CHRON. XI. 1—XX. 8.

1. *Call to the kingdom over Judah*, 2 Sam. i–ii. 4: *a.* Amalekite's report of Saul's death; *b.* David's sorrow and lament in book of *Jashar*—analyze this song; *c.* Jehovah commands David to go up to Hebron; *d.* anointed king over house of Judah; *e.* David's kindness to Saul's remains (cf. also 2 Sam. xxi. 12–14).

1

2. *Dual kingdom attempted*, 2 Sam. ii. 8 sq.: *a.* Abner anoints Ish-bosheth king over Israel at Mahanaim; *b.* war between Joab, of Judah, and Abner, of Israel, at pool of Gibeon—result? *c.* David became stronger, house of Saul weaker; *d.* peace between Abner and David; *e.* treachery of Joab, murder and burial of Abner; *f.* weakness and murder of Ish-bosheth; *g.* David's punishment of the murderers.

3. *David king over all Israel, in Jerusalem*, 2 Sam. v., vi; 1 Chron. xi., xii., xiv: *a.* David made king by all Israel in Hebron; *b.* his army in Hebron, 1 Chron. xi. 10—xii. 40; *c.* his conquest of Jebus; *d.* relations to Hiram of Tyre; *e.* David's polygamy; *f.* victories over the Philistines.

4. *Establishment of worship in Jerusalem*, 2 Sam. vi; 1 Chron. xiii., xv: *a.* ark to Jerusalem: (1) from Kirjath-jearim to house of Obed-edom, (2) fatality to Uzzah (cf. Num. iii. 29–31; iv. 5, 15, 19, 20), (3) to Jerusalem with music; *b.* sacrifices and blessings of David; *c.* ordination of singers, 1 Chron. xvi. (cf. Pss. cv. 1–15; xcvi. 1–13; cvi. 1, 47, 48).

5. *David's division of labor in the service of Jehovah*, 1 Chron. xxiii—xxvii: *a.* 38,000 Levites: (1) 24,000 to oversee work of house of Jehovah, (2) 6,000 officers and judges, (3) 4,000 door-

keepers, (4) 4,000 musicians; *b.* Asaph, Heman and Jeduthun prophesy with harps, psalteries and cymbals—228 singers, chap. xxv; *c.* doorkeepers, sons of Korah and and Merari; *d.* treasurer—Ahijah; *e.* officers and judges west of Jordan, 1700; *f.* east of Jordan, 2700; *g.* 12 captains, each one month in a year; *h.* princes of 12 tribes; *i.* David's cabinet, xxvii. 25–31.

6. *Nathan's appearance and prophecy*, 2 Sam. vii; 1 Chron. xvii: *a.* Nathan's own advice annulled by Jehovah; *b.* David's seed to build a house to Jehovah; *c.* David's throne to be established forever; *d.* David's humble prayer.

7. *David's foreign conquests*, 2 Sam. viii; 1 Chron. xviii: *a.* Philistines, viii. 1; *b.* Moab, viii. 2; *c.* Hadadezer of Zobah, viii. 3–8: (1) Syrians, (2) Betah and Berothai, of Hadadezer; *d.* Toi of Hamath; *e.* Edom.

8. *David's kindness to the house of Saul*, 2 Sam. ix.

9. *Provoked foreign wars*, 2 Sam. x., xi. 1; 1 Chron. xix., xx: *a.* Ammon leagued with Syria; *b.* Syria beyond the *river;* *c.* siege of Rabbah, 1 Chron. xx. 1–3; 2 Sam. xii. 26–31.

10. *Locate on the map all places and peoples in this section.*

Literature:

Geikie, Hours, vol. iii. chaps. 8–10.
Blaikie, Manual, chap. 9, sec. 3.
Edersheim, Bible History, vol. iv. chaps. 15–18.
Stanley, Jewish Church, Lec. 23.
Hurlbut, Man. Bib. Geog., pp. 69, 70.
Smith, Old Test. History, chap. 21.
Deane, David, His Life and Times, Men of Bible Series.
Old Test. Student, Oct. 1887.
Taylor, W. M., David, King of Israel, N. Y.
Krummacher, David, King of Israel, Edinburgh, 1867.
Geikie, O. T. Characters, on *David the Psalmist*.
Price, Bibliotheca Sacra, April 1889, on *Book of Jashar*.
Expositor's Bible, Second Samuel.

§54. DAVID'S CALAMITOUS REIGN.—2 SAM. XI. 2—I KINGS II. 11; I CHRON. XXI., XXVII.—XXXI. 30.

1. *David's great sin*, 2 Sam. xi. 2—xii. 31, (*not in Chron.*): *a.* adultery with Bath-sheba; *b.* murder of Uriah; *c.* Bath-sheba becomes David's wife; *d.* Nathan's parable; *e.* David's penitence (cf. Ps. li.); *f.* sorrow at the death his child; *g.* his hope.
2. *Sin in David's household*, 2 Sam. xiii., xiv: *a.*

Amnon's intrigue and sin; *b.* Absalom's feast and murder of Amnon; *c.* flight of Absalom to Geshur; *d.* Joab's scheme and Absalom's return; *e.* David's and Joab's insults to Absalom; *f.* David and Absalom reconciled.

3. *Absalom's revolt and David's flight,* 2 Sam. xv—xvii. 23: *a.* David's part in causing this; *b.* Absalom's device at the gates; *c.* conspiracy at Hebron; *d.* David's flight: (1) Ittai, (2) ark returned, (3) Hushai sent back as a spy, (4) Ziba, (5) Shimei, kin of Saül; *e.* Absalom in Jerusalem: (1) Hushai's deceit, (2) Ahithophel's evil counsel (cf. xvii.1 sq. (3) Hushai's preferred counsel, (4) Ahithophel hangs himself (cf. Judas Iscariot, in Matt. xxvii. 5.)

4. *Battle of the two armies and the result,* 2 Sam. xvii. 24—xix. 43: *a.* Absalom's army under Amasa in Gilead; *b.* David's kind reception at Mahanaim; *c.* charge of David to Joab, Abishai and Ittai, commanders; *d.* battle and death of Absalom; *e.* courier; *f.* David's lament; *g.* Joab rebukes David; *h.* David's return to Jerusalem: (1) David's word to the priests, (2) Shimei, (3) Mephibosheth, (4) Barzillai, (5) the quarrel over David.

5. *Civil war, murder, famine, wars with the Philistines,* 2 Sam. xx., xxi: *a.* Sheba, son of

/

Bichri, slain at Abel; *b.* Joab's murder of Amasa; *c.* famine and demands of Gibeonites; *d.* David's reverence for Saul's remains; *e.* four wars against the Philistines, 2 Sam. xxi. 15–22; 1 Chron. xx. 4–8.

6. *Sin of David in numbering Israel,* 2 Sam. xxiv; 1 Chron. xxi: *a.* Joab's enumeration; *b.* David's conscience smitten; *c.* God's alternatives for David — three years famine, three months defeat, three days pestilence; *d.* David's choice and result; *e.* altar at Ornan's threshing floor.

7. *Usurpation of Adonijah,* 1 Kings i: *a.* Adonijah's retinue; *b.* made king by some (vss. 11, 18); *c.* deserted by the people; *d.* submission to Solomon.

8. *David's final assemblage of Israel,* 1 Chron. xxviii–xxix. 25: *a.* review of God's favor and promises; *b.* charge to Solomon to build the temple; *c.* enumeration of materials, chaps. xxii. and xxviii. 11–21; *d.* plan of the building and its vessels; *e.* after David's example, people offer willingly large sums; *f.* David's prayer of praise and thanksgiving; *g.* people bless, and offer sacrifice to God; *h.* David's successor to be Solomon.

9. *David's final charge to Solomon, and his death,* 1 Kings ii. 1–11; 1 Chron. xxix. 26–30: *a.* to obey Jehovah; *b.* take vengeance on (*1*)

Joab, (2) Shimei; *c.* to care for sons of Barzillai; *d.* death and burial of David in the city of David; *e.* ruled seven years in Hebron, thirty-three in Jerusalem.

10. *Give an estimate of David's character as: a.* warrior; *b.* king; *c.* man; *d.* writer.

Literature:

Geikie, Hours, vol. iii. chaps. 11–13.
Blaikie, Manual, chap. 9, sec. 3.
Edersheim, Bible History, vol. iv. chap. 19; vol. v. chaps. 1–3.
Stanley, Jewish Church, Lec. 24.
Hurlbut, Man. of Bib. Geog., pp. 70, 71.
Smith, Old Test. History, chap. 21.
David, His Life and Times, Men of Bible Series.
Old Test. Student, Oct. 1887.
Taylor, W. M., David, King of Israel.
Krummacher, David, King of Israel.

§55. THE REIGN OF SOLOMON.—I KINGS I—XI; 2 CHRON. I—IX.

1. *Coronation and charge*, see §54, 9.
2. *Fate of:* a. Adonijah; *b.* Abiathar; *c.* Joab; *d.* Shimei.
3. *Visions at Gibeon*, 1 Kings iii. 4–15; 2 Chron. i. 1–13: I. *a.* kind of high-place; *b.* object of their presence there; *c.* Solomon's request of Jehovah; *d.* Jehovah's promise; *e.* celebration of this event at Jerusalem. II. significance and purport of the second vision.

4. *Solomon's wisdom:* a. extensive, world-wide, 1 Kings iv. 34; v. 7, 12; x. 23, 24; 2 Chron. ix. 22, 23; b. in scientific and literary knowledge, 1 Kings iv. 29–34; c. in dealing with hard questions, 1 Kings x. 1–8; 2 Chron. ix. 1–7; d. in dealing with practical questions, 1 Kings iii. 9, 11, 12, 16–28.

5. *Solomon's foreign domestic alliances:* a. Pharaoh's daughter, 1 Kings iii. 1; vii. 8; ix. 16, 24; xi. 1; 2 Chron. viii. 11; b. women of Moabites, Ammonites, Edomites, Zidonians and Hittites, 1 Kings xi. 1; c. Naamah, mother of Rehoboam, an Ammonitess, 1 Kings xiv. 21, 31; d. alliances of Solomon's daughters, iv. 11, 15; e. purpose of Solomon in all these alliances; f. actual result for Solomon and for the kingdom.

6. *Solomon's government:* a. slaves not Israelites, 1 Kings ix. 22, 21; 2 Chron. viii. 7, 8; burden bearers in the mountains, 2 Chron. ii. 17, 18, 2; 1 Kings v. 13–18; b. commissary department, (*1*) twelve divisions, (*2*) service one month, (*3*) provisions for one day, 1 Kings iv. 22, 23, (*4*) other duties, 1 Kings iv. 26–28; c. superintendents of work, (*1*) "3,300 bare rule over workers in the mountains," 1 Kings v. 16 (cf. 2 Chron. ii. 2, 18); (*2*) 550 chief officers, 1 Kings ix. 23: v. 16 (cf. 2 Chron. viii. 10); d. cabinet, 1 Kings iv. 1–6;

e. army, horses and chariots, 1 Kings iv. 26, 28; 2 Chron. i. 14; ix. 25, 28 (cf. Deut. xvii. 16); *f.* extent of his dominions, 1 Kings iv. 21, 24; 2 Chron. ix. 26; *g.* prophecy regarding it.

7. *Foreign commercial relations*: *a.* Egypt and Hittites—horses and chariots, 1 Kings x. 28, 29; 2 Chron. i. 16, 17; ix. 28; also out of all lands, 2 Chron. ix. 28; *b.* Phœnicia, building materials and skilled labor, 1 Kings v. 6, 8-12; ix. 11-14; 2 Chron. ii. 8-16; *c.* voyages—sea trade, 1 Kings ix. 26-28; x. 11, 12, 22; 2 Chron. viii. 17, 18; ix. 10, 11, 21; *d.* general trade, 1 Kings x. 15; 2 Chron. ix. 14 (cf. 1 Kings x. 1-13); *e.* commercial cities, 1 Kings ix. 18; 2 Chron. viii. 4.

NOTE—What were ships of Tarshish? course, destination, etc.? cf. 1 Kings ix. 28, with 2 Chron. viii. 18.

8. *Solomon's revenues—immense:* *a.* gold and silver, 1 Kings x. 14, 15; 2 Chron. ix. 13, 14; *b.* levies of provisions, 1 Kings iv. 7-28; *c.* presents, 1 Kings iv. 21; x. 1-10, 13, 23-25; 2 Chron. ix. 22-24; *d.* tropical products, 1 Kings x. 22, etc.; 2 Chron. ix. 21; *e.* slave-service, see 6. *a.* above.

9. *Increase in culture:* *a.* learning and literature, 1 Kings iv. 29-34; x. 23, 24; 2 Chron. ix. 22, 23 (read Geikie, vol. iii. 18); *b.* architecture, see §56; *c.* decorations, read 1 Kings vi-vii; *d.* general splendor of courts, 1 Kings x. 1-13.

10. *Solomon's old age and death:* a. polygamy, 1 Kings xi. 1–3; b. idolatry, kinds of foreign deities, 1 Kings xi. 4–8; c. Jehovah's word against him; d. his new enemies, 1 Kings xi. 9–25; e. Ahijah's prophecy and Jeroboam's flight, 1 Kings xi. 26–40; f. death of Solomon; g. length of his reign.
11. *Solomon's career and character:* a. politically; b. religiously; c. intellectually.

Literature:

Geikie, Hours, vol. iii. chaps. 14, 15, 17.
Blaikie, Manual, chap. 9, secs. 4 and 5.
Edersheim, Bible History, vol. v. chaps. 4 and 5, 8 and 9.
Stanley, Jewish Church, Lec. 26.
Solomon, his Life and Times, Men of Bible Series.
Hurlbut, Man. Bib. Geog., p. 71.
Old Test. Student, Dec. 1887.
Smith, Old Test. History, chap. 22.
Geikie, Old Test. Characters, on *Solomon*, *The Queen of Sheba*.

§56. SOLOMON'S TEMPLE.*

1. *Steps up to the temple:* a. offering, Gen. iv. 3, 4; b. altar, Gen. viii. 20; xii. 6–8 (cf. Ex. xx. 24, 25); c. "house of God"—Bethel, Gen. xxviii. 18–22; xxxv. 1–3, 6, 14, 15; d. "tent

---

*This outline is a revision of that of Dr. Hurlbut as given in Old Test. Student, Dec. 1887.

of meeting"—Tabernacle, Ex. xxv. 8; xxix. 42–45, *e.* "temple" in Shiloh, 1 Sam. i. 9; iii. 3.

2. *Building of the temple:* *a.* place, Mt. Moriah in Jerusalem, Gen. xxii. 1, 2, 14; bought by David, 2 Sam. xxiv. 17–25; 1 Chron. xxi. 18–30; xxii. 1 (cf. 2 Chron. iii. 1); *b.* foundation—extended 270 feet over arches, concealing reservoirs of water (cf. Ps. xlvi. 1–5); *c.* materials—provided largely by David, 2 Sam. vi. 1–12; vii. 1–13; 1 Chron. xxviii. 11–19; xxix. 2–8; (*1*) stone; (*2*) iron, 1 Chron. xxii. 14; xxix. 2; (*3*) cedar wood, 2 Chron. ii. 3–9; 1 Kings vi. 8–10; (*4*) silver and gold, 1 Chron. xxii. 14; xxix. 4; (*5*) brass, or bronze, 1 Chron. xxix. 2; 1 Kings vii. 15–17; (*6*) precious stones, 1 Chron. xxix. 2; *d.* construction: (*1*) under Phœnician workmen, 1 Kings vii. 13 sq., 40–45; 2 Chron. iv. 11–16; (*2*) no sound of hammer or iron tool, 1 Kings vi. 7 (cf. Deut. xxvii. 5, 6); (*3*) completed in seven years and six months, 1 Kings vi. 1, 38.

3. *Plan of the temple:* *a.* twice the size of the tabernacle, for the most part, cf. Ex. xxv–xl; 1 Kings v–viii; 2 Chron. iii–vii (cf. Ezekiel's vision, Ezek. xl–xlvi); *b.* parts: 1) *court*, (cf. Ex. xxvii. 9–18); 1 Kings viii. 64; 2 Chron. xx. 5; xxiv. 21; outer and inner, 1 Kings vi.

36; 2 Chron. iv. 9; (*a*) *inner* more sacred, Joel ii. 17; (*b*) *outer* had (*1*) *altar*, 2 Chron. iv. 1; (*2*) *sea of brass* on 12 oxen, 2 Chron. iv. 2-5; (*3*) *ten lavers*, 2 Chron. iv. 6; 1 Kings vii. 27-39; (*4*) perhaps a *grove of trees*, Ps. lii. 8; xcii. 12-14; 2) *porch*—vestibule—180 ft. high, 2 Chron. iii. 4; pillars Jachin and Boaz at the entrance, 1 Kings vii. 15-22; 3) *holy place*—"greater house," 2 Chron. iii. 5; 1 Kings vi. 17; (*a*) ten candlesticks, 2 Chron. iv. 7; (*b*) ten tables, 2 Chron. iv. 8; (*c*) double doors, 1 Kings vi. 31-33; (*d*) altar of incense, 1 Kings vii. 48; 2 Chron. iv. 19; 4) *holy of holies*—"the oracle," 1 Kings vi. 16; 2 Chron. iii. 8; (*a*) cherubim, 2 Chron. iii. 10-13; (*b*) ark of the covenant, 2 Chron. v. 4-10 (cf. Ex. xxv. 10-22); 5) *chambers*—for priests—three stories high, 1 Kings vi. 5-10; Jer. xxxvi. 10; Ezek. xl. 45, 46; xlii. 1-6.

4. *Purpose of the temple:* a. to centralize and locate public worship of Jehovah (cf. Ps. lxxxiv); *b*. to bind together the tribes—one altar, one shrine, others forbidden, Deut. xii. 8-14; Josh. xxii. 10-27; Deut, xvi. 16; 1 Kings xii. 26-28; *c*. to symbolize the truths of redemption, cf. Lev. i. 1-5; 2 Chron. vii. 1-14; Heb. ix. 22; *d*. to symbolize the presence of Jehovah among his people, cf. Ex. xx. 3, 4; Lev. xxvi. 11, 12; 2 Chron. vi. 1, 2.

5. *History of Solomon's temple:* a. dedication, (*1*) assembly, (*2*) offerings, (*3*) Solomon's prayer, 1 Kings viii.; 2 Chron. v. 1–6, b. popular regard for the temple, Pss. xxvii. 4; xliii. 1–4; cxxxii. 1–5; c. plundered by Shishak of Egypt under Rehoboam, 2 Chron. xii. 9–11; d. repairs under Joash, 2 Kings xii. 4–15; e. desecration and plunder by Ahaz, 2 Kings xvi. 10–19; f. repairs by Hezekiah, 2 Chron. xxix; g. desecration by Manasseh, 2 Chron. xxxiii. 1–18; h. purification and repairs by Josiah, 2 Chron. xxxiv. 1–13, 29–33; i. destruction by Nebuchadrezzar, 2 Chron. xxxvi. 11–21; Jer. lii. 12–23.

Literature:

Geikie, Hours, vol. iii. chap. 16.
Edersheim, Bible History, vol. v. chaps. 6 and 7.
Solomon's Temple, plan in Hurlbut Man. Bib. Geog., p. 71.
Stanley, Jewish Church, Lec. 27.
Old Test. Student, Dec. 1887.
Solomon, His Life and Times, Men of the Bible, chap. 8.
Perrot and Chipiez, Le Temple Jerusalem restitutes, Paris, 1889.

NINTH PERIOD.

DUAL KINGDOM. DIVISION TO FALL OF SAMARIA. B. C. 975–722.

§57. DUAL RELIGIOUS DECLINE.—I KINGS XI. 26 —XV. 8; 2 CHRON. X–XIII.

Judah—Rehoboam (17)*, Abijam (3).
Israel—Jeroboam J (22).

1. *Prophecies of disruption*, 1 Kings xi. 9–13, 29–39.
2. *Causes of disruption: a.* mediate: (*1*) old animosities between kingdoms of Saul and David, (*2*) Solomon's foreign domestic alliances, (*3*) Solomon's idolatry, 1 Kings xi. 9–13; *b.* immediate: (*1*) Ahijah's encouragement to Jeroboam, (*2*) Rehoboam's outrageous requests.
3. *Events immediately connected with disruption*, 2 Chron. x; 1 Kings xii. 1–19: *a.* Rehoboam at Shechem; *b.* request of the people; *c.* counsel adopted by Rehoboam; *d.* Jeroboam's appearance.
4. *Kingdom divided: a.* Solomon's empire—60,000 square miles; *b.* portions sliced off by ene-

---

* Henceforth these numbers shall indicate the length of reign of the kings after whose names they stand.

mies; *c.* territory of northern kingdom, 9,400 square miles; *d.* territory of Judah, 3,400 square miles.

5. *Jeroboam's establishment and policy*, 1 Kings xii. 20—xiii. 34: *a.* coronation; *b.* army and defences; *c.* system of worship, its localities and purpose (cf. 2 Chron. xiii. 9); *d.* rebuke and prophecy (cf. 1 Kings xiii. 2 with 2 Kings xxiii. 16) of man of God.

6. *Jeroboam's fate foretold*, 1 Kings xiv: *a.* sickness of Abijah; *b.* secret march on Ahijah; *c.* Ahijah foretells, (*1*) death of Abijah, (*2*) destruction of Jeroboam's house, (*3*) captivity of Israel.

7. *Rehoboam's establishment and policy*, 1 Kings xiv. 21–24; 2 Chron. xi: *a.* coronation; *b.* attempt to suppress revolt; *c.* defences, 2 Chron. xi. 5–12; *d.* accessions from Israel, 2 Chron. xi. 13–17; *e.* sins of his house, 18–23.

8. *Invasion by Shishak of Egypt*, 1 Kings xiv. 25–28; 2 Chron. xii. 2–9: *a.* Solomon's early relations with Egypt; *b.* probable provocation of Shishak; *c.* extent of his plunderings; *d.* humility of Rehoboam; *e.* death of Rehoboam; *f.* character of Rehoboam.

9. *Career of Abijam*, 1 Kings xv. 1–8; 2 Chron. xiii: *a.* walked in sins of his father; *b.* railed against Jeroboam; *c.* warred against Jero-

boam, 400,000 against 800,000 respectively; *d.* Abijam victorious; *e.* Jehovah smote him and he died; *f.* characterize him.

10. *Locate all geographical points in this section.*
11. *Contemporaneous history:* a. Syria; b. Egypt; c. Assyria; d. Hittites.
12. *Prophets of these times:* I. Judah: *a.* Shemaiah, his work, 2 Chron. xi. 2; xii. 15; 1 Kings xii. 22, 23; *b.* "man of God out of Judah," 1 Kings xiii. 1, 5, 6, 7, 8; *c.* Iddo, 2 Chron. xii. 15; xiii. 22. II. Israel: *a.* Ahijah the Shilonite, 1 Kings· xi. 29, 30; xii. 15; xiv. 2–16; *b.* old prophet, 1 Kings xiii. 11–31.

Literature:

Geikie, Hours, vol. iv. chap. 1.
Blaikie, Manual, chap. 10, sec. 1; chap. 11, secs. 1 and 2.
Edersheim, Bible History, vol. v. chaps. 10 and 11.
Stanley, Jewish Church, Lecs. 29 and half of 35.
Rawlinson, Kings of Israel and Judah, chaps. 1, 2.
Hurlbut, Man. Bib. Geog., pp. 87, 88.
Old Test. Student, Jan. 1888.
Smith, O. T. History, chap. 23.
Geikie, O. T. Characters, on *Rehoboam.*
Sayce, The Hittites, Religious Tract Society.

§58. { REIGN OF ASA IN JUDAH.
{ FALL OF THREE DYNASTIES IN ISRAEL.
B. C. 955-915.

Judah—Asa (41).
Israel—Jeroboam (22), Nadab (2), Baasha (24), Elah (2), Zimri (7 days).
1 Kings xv. 8–xvii. 20; 2 Chron. xiv–xvi.

1. *Review briefly the events since the disruption.*
2. *Reforms of Asa:* I. Religious: *a.* removing Sodomites and idols; *b.* breaking down high places, pillars; *c.* his queen-mother removed; *d.* groves of Asherim cut down; *e.* Israel bade to seek Jehovah; *f.* brought dedicated things into house of Jehovah. II. Political: *a.* fortified Judah; *b.* built cities; *c.* strengthened the army.
3. *Aids to these reforms:* *a.* counter-example of Israel; *b.* immigration to Judah of those loyal to Jehovah; *c.* presence of the prophets; *d.* spirit of Jehovah in Asa's heart.
4. *Asa's wars and alliances:* *a.* victorious battle with Ethiopia, 580,000 men against 1,000,000 men; *b.* Baasha of Israel builds Ramah; *c.* Syria, Ben-hadad of Damascus bought off by Asa with vessels of the temple; *d.* disposal of Ramah.
5. *Asa's relations with the prophets, and the end of his days:* *a.* Azariah, son of Oded, result to Asa and Israel, 2 Chron. xv. 1–7; *b.* Hanani

1

the seer, result, 2 Chron. xvi. 7-10; *c.* disease of Asa; *d.* death and burial; *e.* length of reign.
6. *Nadab's character, reign and death*, 1 Kings xv. 25-31: *a.* second and last king of dynasty of Jeroboam; *b.* began in second year of Asa; *c.* did evil as his father; *d.* slain by Baasha at the siege of Gibbethon.
7. *Baasha's character, reign and death*, 1 Kings xv. 27-xvi. 13; 2 Chron. xvi. 1-6: *a.* usurper; *b.* began to reign in the third year of Asa, in city of Tirzah; *c.* did evil as Jeroboam; *d.* destroyed all the house of Jeroboam; *e.* in his fourteenth year he fortified Ramah against Judah; *f.* Ben-hadad's inroads on Israel; *g.* Jehu's prophecy against Baasha; *h.* died and buried in Tirzah; *i.* length of reign.
8. *Elah's character, reign and death*, 1 Kings xvi. 6-14: *a.* second and last king of dynasty of Baasha; *b.* began to reign in 26th year of Asa; *c.* made Israel to sin, 1 Kings xvi. 12, 13; *d.* slain in a drunken row at Tirzah by Zimri; *e.* length of reign.
9. *Zimri's (7 days) reign and death*, 1 Kings xvi. 9-20: *a.* usurper—third dynasty; *b.* obliterated house of Baasha; *c.* choice of people was Omri, captain at Gibbethon; *d.* siege of Tirzah, and suicide of Zimri after seven days' reign; *e.* similar suicides in secular history.

10. *Locate all geographical points in this section.*
11. *Contemporaneous history:* a. Ethiopia; b. Syria; c. Assyria.
12. *Prophets of this section:* I. Judah: a. Azariah, son of Oded, 2 Chron. xv. 1–7; b. Hanani the seer, 2 Chron. xvi. 7–10. II. Israel: Jehu son of Hanani, 1 Kings xvi. 1.

Literature:

Geikie, Hours, vol. iv. chap. 2 in part.
Blaikie, Manual, chap. 10, sec. 2.
Edersheim, Bible History, vol. v. chaps. 12, and 13 in part.
Stanley, Jewish Church, half of Lec. 35.
Rawlinson, Kings of Israel and Judah, Men of Bible Series, chaps. 4–8.
Hurlbut, Man. Bib. Geog., pp. 87, 88.
Old Test. Student, Jan. 1888.

§59. REIGN OF THE HOUSE OF OMRI IN ISRAEL, B. C. 929–885.

Omri (12), Ahab (22), Ahaziah (2), Jehoram (12).

1. *Give the kings of Israel in the last three dynasties with length of reigns.*
2. *Omri's reign and home policy*, 1 Kings xvi. 16–29: a. usurper; b. began 27th year of Asa; c. right disputed by Tibni, four years; d. his capitals, (*1*) Tirzah, (*2*) Samaria; e.

religious policy, (*1*) advance on Jeroboam, I Kings xvi. 25; (*2*) statutes adopted, Mic. vi. 16.*

3. *Omri's foreign relations, power and death:* a. with Moab, reduced Mesha, (cf. Records of Past, 2d series, vol. ii., p. 200 sq. and 2 Kings iii. 4); *b.* with Syria, when king of Syria wrested cities from Omri, I Kings xx. 34; *c.* with Zidonians, inferred from tradition and Ahab's alliance; *d.* with Assyria, land of Israel, called "Land of Omri" for several generations; *e.* evidence of power, the location of his new capital; *f.* his death; *g.* length of reign.

4. *Ahab's beginning, 38th year of Asa,* I Kings xvi. 29—xvii. 1: *a.* alliance with Zidonians through Jezebel; *b.* new religion introduced, its character; *c.* persecution of servants of Jehovah; *d.* Ahab's advance religiously, I Kings xvi. 31, 33; *e.* Elijah's prophecy of famine.

5. *Ahab's course at home,* I Kings xviii., xxi: I. *a.* despair in famine; *b.* Elijah's appearance and Obadiah; *c.* Ahab's salute; *d.* Elijah's assembly at Carmel; *e.* Ahab's prophets' vain attempt; *f.* Elijah's success and slaughter; *g.* rain; *h.* Jezebel's wrath, and pursuit of Elijah; *i.* public works of Ahab,

---

*Cf. also 2 Kings viii. 26.

1 Kings xxii. 39. II. Naboth's vineyard: *a.* Ahab's request; *b.* refused by Naboth; *c.* Ahab's pettishness; *d.* Jezebel's infamy; *e.* justice satisfied; *f.* law of inheritance; *g.* Elijah at hand; *h.* Ahab's penitence; *i.* Elijah's last message to Ahab.

6. *Ahab's foreign relations and wars*, 1 Kings xx., xxii; 2 Chron. xviii.: *a.* with Zidon and the Phœnicians; *b.* with Ben-hadad of Syria: (*1*) before Samaria: (*a*) with 32 allied kings, (*b*) completely routed; (*2*) at Aphek: (*a*) Ben-hadad routed, (*b*) saved, why? (*c*) Ahab rebuked by son of a prophet; *c.* with Assyrians, at Karkar (C. O. T., vol. i., pp. 182–195), Ahab in league with several kings, defeated by Shalmaneser II; *d.* with Jehoshaphat of Judah, against Ramoth Gilead: (*1*) reception at Samaria, (*2*) word of 400 prophets, (*3*) word of Micaiah, (*4*) battle, (*5*) Ahab slain, (*6*) Elijah's prophecy fulfilled, 1 Kings xxi. 19, with xxii. 38; *e.* length of Ahab's reign.

7. *Reign of Ahab's son, Ahaziah,* 1 Kings xxii. 40— 2 Kings i. 18: *a.* alliance with Jehoshaphat; *b.* his sin; *c.* sickness; *d.* inquiry of Baalzebub; *e.* rebuked by Elijah; *f.* fatality of messengers; *g.* Ahaziah's death; *h.* length of reign.

8. *Reign of Ahab's son, Jehoram,* 2 Kings i. 17; iii. 1–27: *a.* religious revolution, 2 Kings iii.

3; *b.* war with Mesha of Moab: (*1*) Jehoshaphat here, (*2*) Elisha's share in it; *c.* Syrians besiege Dothan: (*1*) struck blind, (*2*) well treated and sent home; *d.* Syrians besiege Samaria: (*1*) famine, (*2*) Elisha's word, (*3*) outcome; *e.* disastrous visit of Ahaziah of Judah to Jehoram, after battle of Ramoth Gilead; *f.* length of reign.

9. *Locate with great care all geographical points in this section.*
10. *Contemporaneous history:* *a.* Zidonians or Phœnicians; *b.* Syrians; *c.* Assyrians; *d.* Moabites.
11. *Prophets in Israel in this section:* *a.* Elijah; *b.* Obadiah; *c.* two fifties in caves; *d.* 400 prophets; *e.* Micaiah; *f.* the prophet, 1 Kings xx. 13-22; *g.* man of God, 1 Kings xx. 28; *h.* man of the sons of the prophets, 1 Kings xx. 35.

Literature:

Geikie, Hours, vol. iv. chaps. 2 and 4.
Blaikie, Manual, chap. 10, sec. 3.
Edersheim, Bible History, vol. v. chaps. 14 and 15; vol. vi. chaps. 1, 4, 5, 7, 9.
Stanley, Jewish Church, Lec. 30.
Rawlinson, Kings of Israel and Judah, chaps. 9, 10, 12, 13.
Hurlbut, Man. Bib. Geog., pp. 87, 88.
Old Test. Student, Jan. 1888.

Cuneiform Inscriptions and Old Testament, vol. i. pp. 179–195.
Moabite Stone, in Records of the Past, 2d Series, vol. ii. p. 200 sq.
Smith, Old Test. History, chap. 23 in part.
Geikie, Old Test. Characters, on *Ahab and Jezebel.*

§60. REIGN OF JEHOSHAPHAT OF JUDAH, B. C. 914–889.

1. *Give and characterize the kings of Judah thus far studied.*
2. *Jehoshaphat's beginning*, 1 Kings xv. 24; 2 Chron. xvii: *a.* walked in the first ways of his father David (2 Chron. xvii. 3); *b.* took away Asherim and some high places; *c.* sent princes, priests and Levites to teach the law throughout the cities of the land; *d.* set garrisons in fenced cities of Judah and Ephraim; *e.* increased the army to 1,600,000 men (xvii. 14–19).
3. *Jehoshaphat's relations with Israel*, 1 Kings xxii; 2 Kings iii; 2 Chronicles xviii: *a.* Ahab: (*1*) visit of Jehoshaphat to Samaria, (*2*) league against Syria, (*3*) 400 prophets, (*4*) Micaiah, (*5*) battle of Ramoth Gilead, (*6*) Jehoshaphat on return rebuked by Jehu son of Hanani (2 Chron. xix. 1–3); *b.* Ahaziah son of Ahab: (*1*) common interest in a Tarshish navy, (*2*) Eliezer's rebuke (2 Chron. xx.

37), (*3*) fleet wrecked; *c.* Jehoram son of Ahab: (*1*) against Mesha, king of Moab, (*2*) Judah, Israel and Edom together, (*3*) Elisha's role, (*4*) victory, (*5*) human sacrifice, why did Israel withdraw?
4. *Jehoshaphat's other foreign relations:* a. Arabians and Philistines, peaceful, 2 Chron. xvii. 11; *b.* Moabites, Ammonites, Seir (Syria, 2 Chron. xx. 2) or Edom: (*1*) meet at En-gedi, (*2*) Jehoshaphat's prayer, (*3*) prophecy of Jahaziel, (*4*) song of praise, (*5*) victory without a stroke, (*6*) spoil, (*7*) praise to Jehovah; *c.* Syrians, see 3. *a*; *d.* Mesha of Moab, see 3. *c.*
5. *Close of Jehoshaphat's reign:* a. makes Jehoram his son regent with him, 2 Kings viii. 16: *b.* distributes gifts, gold, silver and fenced cities among his other six sons; *c.* died and buried with his fathers in city of David; *d.* length of reign.
6. *Contrast the characters in these two sections* (§9 and 60), *e.g. Ahab and Jezebel, Ahab and Jehoshaphat.*
7. *Locate all geographical points in this section.*
8. *Prophets in this section:* a. Jehu son of Hanani the seer, 2 Chron. xix. 1-3; *b.* Jahaziel, 2 Chron. xx. 14-17; *c.* Eliezer, 2 Chron. xx. 37.

Literature:

Additional to that under §59: . .   ...
Blaikie, Manual, chap. 11, sec. 2.

Rawlinson, Kings of Israel and Judah, chap. 11.
Geikie, Old Testament Characters, on *Jehoshaphat*.
Edersheim, Bible History, vol. vi. chaps. 5–7, and 9.

§61. THE GREAT PERIOD OF ORAL PROPHETS AND ORAL PROPHECY. B. C. 975–850.

1. *Prophets near the close of Solomon's reign:* a. Ahijah the Shilonite, 2 Chron. ix. 29; 1 Kings xi. 29; *b. Iddo* the seer, 2 Chron. ix. 29.
2. *Minor prophets in the kingdom of Judah, give the work of each:* a. Shemaiah (under Rehoboam 1 Kings xii. 22–24; 2 Chron. xi. 2–4; xii. 5, 7, 15; *b. Iddo* (Rehoboam and Jeroboam), Jeddo or Jedon (Josephus Antiq. viii. 8, 9), 2 Chron. ix. 29; xii. 15; xiii. 22; *c. Azariah* son of Oded (Asa), 2· Chron. xv. 1–8; *d. Hanani* the seer, 2 Chron. xvi. 7–10; *e. Jehu* son of Hanani the seer (Jehoshaphat), 2 Chron. xix. 2, 3; xx. 34; *f. Jahaziel* (Jehoshaphat), 2 Chron. xx. 14–17; *g. Eliezer* (Jehoshaphat), 2 Chron. xx. 37.
3. *Minor prophets in the kingdom of Israel, give the work of each:* a. Ahijah the Shilonite, ((*Solomon*), Jeroboam), 1 Kings xi. 29–39; xii. 15; xiv. 2–18; xv. 29; 2 Chron. ix. 29; x. 15; *b. Iddo,* see 2. *b*; *c. Jehu* son of Hanani (Baasha), 1 Kings xvi, 1–5, 7, 12; *d. Micaiah*

(Ahab), 1 Kings xxii. 8-28; 2 Chron. xviii. 7-27.

NOTE 1.—Iddo and Jehu prophesied in both kingdoms.

NOTE 2.—*Prophet* and *man of God* are frequently mentioned without a hint as to their names; e.g., 1 Kings xiii. 1, 11; xx. 13, 22; 2 Chron. xxv. 7, 15.

4. *Elijah's activity during the famine in Ahab's reign*, 1 Kings xvii., xviii: *a.* his sudden appearance—tribal relations? 1 Kings xvii. 1: *b.* dress, 2 Kings iii. 8; *c.* famine: (*1*) foretold, (*2*) Elijah at Cherith, (*3*) at Zarephath: (*a*) miracle of meal and oil, (*b*) raising dead; (*4*) return and word of Obadiah, (*5*) Ahab's salutation, (*6*) test at Carmel, (*7*) slaughter of prophets of Baal (Deut. xiii. 6-9), (*8*) prayer and rain, (*9*) Elijah runs before Ahab to Jezreel, (*10*) duration of famine, 1 Kings xviii. 1; Luke iv. 25; James v. 17.

5. *Elijah's activity during the remainder of Ahab's reign*, 1 Kings xix., xxi. 17-29: *a.* Elijah's flight before Jezebel: (*1*) Jezebel's threat, (*2*) Elijah in Beer-sheba, (*3*) miraculously fed, (*4*) forty days and nights in Horeb, (*5*) God's manifestation to him, cf. Ex. xxxiii. 21-23, (*6*) commanded to anoint (*a*) Hazael over Syria, (*b*) Jehu over Israel, (*c*) Elisha as his successor; *b.* discovery and mantling of Elisha; *c.* "hast thou found me, O mine enemy?" 1 Kings xxi. 17-20: (*1*) Elijah's message, (*2*)

Ahab's sorrow, (*3*) sentence mitigated.

6. *Elijah's later work:* *a.* rebuked messengers of Ahaziah, 2 Kings i. 3 sq.; *b.* consuming of two fifties; *c.* Elisha's message to Ahaziah; *d.* Elijah's writing to Jehoram of Judah, 2 Chron. xxi. 12–15; *e.* his work among schools of the prophets, 2 Kings ii. 1–7, 15–18; *f.* his appointment of Elisha and his translation.

7. *Elisha's call and work among the sons of the prophets:* *a.* call and conduct, 1 Kings xix. 16–21; *b.* visit with Elijah to the sons of the prophets at Gilgal, Bethel and Jericho; *c.* translation of Elijah, and sons of the prophets at Jericho, (*1*) before, (*2*) after; *d.* healing the waters at Jericho; *e.* to Bethel, bears; *j.* to Carmel; *g.* to Samaria; *h.* miracle of pot of oil, 2 Kings iv. 1 sq.; *i.* Shunem, raising Shunammite's son; *j.* to Gilgal, death in the pot; *k.* multiplying food; *l.* iron swam, 2 Kings vi. 1–7.

8. *Elisha's work of a political or national character:* *a.* in war against Moab, 2 Kings iii. 11–19; *b.* in healing Naaman the Syrian: (*1*) Naaman's source of information, (*2*) his expectation, (*3*) his submission, (*4*) his resolution, (*5*) Gehazi's sin and punishment; *c.* his value to the king of Israel, 2 Kings vi. 8–10; *d.* his fame abroad, 2 Kings vi. 12; *e.* besieged in Dothan, enemy stricken with blind-

ness, feasted, sent home; *f.* Syrians besiege Samaria, 2 Kings vi. 24–vii. 20: (*1*) famine, (*2*) Elisha's prophecy, (*3*) terror strikes the enemy, (*4*) flight of Syrians and plenty for Israel; *g.* Elisha's influence restores Shunammite's property, 2 Kings viii. 1-6; *h.* Elisha's errand at Damascus, 2 Kings viii. 7–15; *i.* anointing of Jehu, 2 Kings ix. 1–12; *j.* Elisha's sickness, prophecy to Joash of Israel, and death, 2 Kings xiii. 14–19; *k.* miracle with bones of Elisha, 2 Kings xiii. 20, 21.

9. *Compare the characters of Elijah and Elisha:* *a.* preparation for work; *b.* habits of life; *c.* force of character; *d.* relations to rulers; *e.* relation to sons of prophets.

10. *Schools of the sons of the prophets:** *a.* headquarters: (*1*) Ramah, (*2*) Bethel, (*3*) Gilgal, (*4*) Jericho, (*5*) Carmel, (*6*) Samaria; *b.* teachers: (*1*) Samuel, 1 Sam. xix. 20, (*2*) Elijah, (*3*) Elisha; *c.* things taught, (*1*) prophesying, (*2*) sacred service and music; *d.* occupation, (*1*) study and worship, (*2*) run errands, (*3*) regular duties of a prophet; *e.* means of subsistence: (*1*) gathered in fields, (2) gifts, 2 Kings iv. 42, 43; v. 21–24.

11. *Work of the prophets:* *a.* to instruct the people in the law; *b.* to convey the direct will of God, mostly upon occasions of great moment;

---

*This topic is fully treated by the author in Old Testament Stuent, March 1889.

c. to forewarn and admonish rulers; *d.* to embody in written form their instructions direct from God; *e.* to preserve a history of their times†; *f.* to counteract all idolatrous tendencies; *g.* to provide music, etc., at public religious services, 1 Chron. xxv.

Remark.—False prophets: I. *a.* old prophet of Bethel, 1 Kings xiii. 11; *b.* 400 prophets with a lying spirit, 1 Kings xxii. 6–8, 22, 23; *c.* 450 prophets of Baal, 1 Kings xviii. 19, 22, 40; *d.* 400 prophets of Asherah, 1 Kings xviii. 19. II. *a.* are they idolatrous prophets? *b.* are they perverted worshippers of Jehovah, wicked men? *c.* do they really predict? *d.* their methods and means of procedure.

Literature:

2 Sam. i—2 Kings xiii. 20.
2 Chron. ix. 29—xx. 37.
Geikie, Hours, vol. iv. chaps. 3 and 5.
Blaikie, Manual, chap. 10, sec. 3.
Edersheim, Bible History, vol. iv. chaps. 1–3, 10–14.
Stanley, Jewish Church, Lecs. 29–31.
Elijah, His Life and Times, Men of Bible Series.
Geikie, O. T. Characters, on *Elijah, Elisha, Naaman the Syrian.*
Old Test. Student, Jan. 1887.

---

† Several of the prophets mentioned in this section wrote works, not one of which exists at the present day. -- This subject is discussed by the author in the Bibliotheca Sacra, April 1889, under the title, "The Lost Writings quoted and referred to in the Old Testament."

1

Price, The Schools of the Sons of the Prophets, Old Test. Student, March 1889.
Price, The Lost Writings in the Old Testament, Bibliotheca Sacra, April 1889.
Howat, Elijah the Desert Prophet, Edinburgh, 1868.

§62. { RELIGIOUS DECLINE IN JUDAH.
      { CHECK TO IDOLATRY IN ISRAEL.

B. C. ca. 890—ca. 840.

Judah—Jehoram (8), Ahaziah (1), Athaliah (7), Joash (40).
Israel—Jehu (28), Jehoahaz (17).

1. *Reign of Jehoram of Judah*, 2 Kings viii. 16–24; 2 Chron. xxi. 1–20: *a.* regent with his father, 2 Kings viii. 16; *b.* slew his brethren—why? 2 Chron. xxi. 1–4; *c.* daughter of Jezebel to wife, 2 Kings viii. 18; *d.* walked in ways of kings of Israel; *e.* revolt of Edomites—why? *f.* revolt of Libnah; *g.* high places made; *h.* letter from Elijah; *i.* Jehoram's disease; *j.* raid of the Philistines and Arabians, result; *k.* ignominious death and burial; *l.* length of reign.

2. *Reign of Ahaziah of Judah*, 2 Kings viii. 24–29; ix. 16–28; 2 Chron. xxii. 1–9: *a.* Ahaziah's legacy, blood of Jezebel; *b.* walked in ways of Ahab, by counsel; *c.* leagues with Jehoram, his uncle, against Ramoth Gilead; *d.* Jehoram wounded; *e.* Ahaziah's visit to Jezreel.

3. *Jehu's extirpation of the house of Omri*, 2 Kings ix—x. 17; 2 Chron. xxii. 7–9: *a.* anointing and coronation of Jehu at Ramoth Gilead, 2 Kings ix. 1–15; *b.* his explicit orders; *c.* haste to Jezreel, vss. 16–20; *d.* murder of Jehoram, 21–26; *e.* murder of Ahaziah of Judah, 27–29; *f.* death of Jezebel, 30–37; *g.* murder of Ahab's seventy sons in Samaria, 2 Kings x. 1–9; *h.* murder of Ahab's kinsfolk, great men and friends, 10–11; *i.* murder of forty-two of Ahaziah's brethren, 12–14; *j.* slaughter of all that remained of Ahab in Samaria.

NOTE—Jehonadab son of Rechab (cf. Jer. xxxv.)

4. *Jehu's stroke at idolatry*, 2 Kings x. 11, 18–28: *a.* murder of priests of Ahab, x. 11; *b.* slaughter of Baal worshippers, 18–25; *c.* obelisks, pillar and house of Baal destroyed; *d.* but the calves of Jeroboam retained.

5. *Jehu's enemies and death*, 2 Kings x. 29–36: *a.* his own heart, (*1*) in unwarranted wholesale murder, (*2*) in sins of Jeroboam; *b.* Hazael of Syria, x. 32, 33; *c.* Assyria, his tribute thereto (C. O. T. vol. i. p. 199 sq.); *d.* Jehovah's promise to Jehu; *e.* death and burial in Samaria; *f.* length of reign.

6. *Athaliah's usurpation, reign and death*, 2 Kings xi; 2 Chron. xxii. 10—xxiii. 21: *a.* ancestry, Jezebel; *b.* bloody disposal of seed royal—except Joash; *c.* Baal worship in the lead.

2 Kings xi. 18; 2 Chron. xxiii. 17; xxiv. 7; *d.* rise and influence of Jehoiada; *e.* assembly and coronation of Joash; *f.* Athaliah slain.

7. *Prosperous reign of Joash of Judah,* 2 Kings xi. 2, 12—xii. 16; 2 Chron. xxii. 11; xxiii. 11—xxiv. 16: *a.* concealment; *b.* accession; *c.* in seventh year of Jehu; *d.* did right; *e.* repairs of house of Jehovah; *f.* Jehoiada's prominent role; *g.* Jehoiada's death and burial.

8. *Disastrous reign of Joash of Judah,* 2 Kings xii. 17-21; 2 Chron. xxiv. 17-27: *a.* princes influential with the king; *b.* house of Jehovah forsaken; *c.* prophets unheeded; *d.* Zechariah, by king's demand, stoned; *e.* invasion of the Syrians; *f.* Hazael bought off by temple plunder; *g.* Joash's disgraceful murder and burial; *h.* length of reign.

9. *Reign of Jehoahaz (son of Jehu) of Israel,* 2 Kings xiii. 1-9: *a.* began 23d year of Joash of Judah; *b.* did evil as Jeroboam; *c.* was delivered up to Hazael and Ben-hadad of Syria; *d.* besought Jehovah; *e.* delivered but weakened (cf. 2 Kings xiii. 23); *f.* death and burial in Samaria; *g.* length of reign.

10. *Carefully point out all geographical points in this section.*

11. *Contemporaneous history:* *a.* Edomites' revolt; *b.* raid of Philistines and Arabians; *c.* Syria:

(*1*) Ramoth Gilead, (*2*) Gath, (*3*) Jerusalem; *d.* Assyria.

12. *Prophets of this section:* I. Judah: *a.* Elijah; *b.* Zechariah. II. Israel: *a.* Elisha; *b.* son of the prophets.

Literature:

Geikie, Hours, vol. iv. chap. 6.
Blaikie, Manual, chap. 10, sec. 4; chap. 11, sec. 3.
Edersheim, Bible History, vol. vi. chaps. 15–17; vol. vii. chaps. 1–3.
Stanley, Jewish Church, Lec. 32.
Rawlinson, Kings of Israel and Judah, chaps. 14–19.
Old Testament Student, Jan. 1888.
Geikie, Old Testament Characters, on *Athaliah*, *Jehu*.
Smith, Old Test. History, chap. 23.
Sayce, Fresh Light from the Ancient Monuments.
Cuneiform Inscrip. and Old Test. vol. i. p. 199 sq.

§63. RELIGIOUS DECLINE AND REGAL PROSPERITY.

B. C. 840–ca. 760.

Judah— Amaziah (29), Uzziah (52).
Israel—Joash (16), Jeroboam II (41), Zechariah (6m.).

1. *Give kings of Israel and Judah to this point, with length of reign of each.*
2. *Reign of Joash (son of Jehoahaz) of Israel,* 2 Kings xiii. 9—xiv. 1, 8–16; 2 Chron. xxv. 17–24: *a.* departed not from sins of Jero-

boam, son of Nebat; *b.* visit to Elisha's death-bed, result; *c.* in three victories he recovered cities from Syria; *d.* Amaziah's challenge; *e.* Joash's victory, plunder and breaking down the walls of Jerusalem; *f.* hostages taken; *g.* death and burial in Samaria.

3. *Reign of Amaziah (son of Joash) of Judah*, 2 Kings xiv. 1–22; 2 Chron. xxv: *a.* did right, *yet not* as David; *b.* slew his father's murderers (see §62; 8 *g.*); *c.* army, 300,000; *d.* 100,000 hired from Israel; *e.* rebuked by a *man of God*, Amaziah sends them back; *f.* their anger and raid of Judah's cities; *g.* victory over Edom: (*1*) 10.000 slain, (*2*) 10,000 cast from top of a rock; *h.* gods of Edom brought home, set up and worshipped; *i.* rebuked by *a prophet*; *j.* challenges Joash of Israel; *k.* Amaziah disastrously defeated; *l.* slain by a conspiracy in Lachish.

4. *Reign of Jeroboam II of Israel*, 2 Kings xiii. 13; xiv. 16, 23–29; xv. 1: *a.* did evil in sight of Jehovah, as Jeroboam I; *b.* restored border of Israel from entering in of Hamath to the sea of the Arabah (Dead Sea); *c.* all according to Jonah's prophecy, 2 Kings xiv. 25; *d.* Jeroboam II Israel's helper; *e.* recovered Damascus; *f.* had great power and prosperity; *g.* death and burial in Samaria.

5. *Condition of Israel at close of Jeroboam's reign:* *a.* territorially next to Solomon; *b.* living luxuriously, Amos iii. 12; vi. 8, 11, 14; *c.* in low state of morals, Hos. iv. 13; Amos ii. 7; iv. 1-8; viii. 12; *d.* fraudulent oppression, Hos. v. 1; Amos iii. 9; *e.* nearing state of dissolution, Amos iii. 12; v. 27; vii. 17.

6. *Reign of Zechariah (son of Jeroboam II) of Israel*, 2 Kings xv. 8-12: *a.* began 38th year of Uzziah; *b.* "did as his fathers had done"; *c.* last of dynasty of Jehu, smitten after six months reign by Shallum, a conspirator; *d.* promise to Jehu fulfilled, 2 Kings x. 30.

7. *Reign of Uzziah (Azariah) of Judah, politically*, 2 Kings xiv. 21, 22; xv. 1-7; 2 Chron. xxvi: *a.* built Elath and restored it to Judah; *b.* began, 16 years old, in 27th year of Jeroboam II; *c.* conquered Philistines; *d.* defeated Arabians in Gur-baal; *e.* Ammonites submissive; *f.* fame gone down to Egypt; *g.* fortified Jerusalem; *h.* improved the country; *i.* practiced husbandry; *j.* standing army 307,500; *k.* new weapons, offensive and defensive; *l.* power famous abroad; *m.* God made him to prosper as long as he sought him.

8. *Reign of Uzziah (Azariah) of Judah, religiously:* *a.* did right as Amaziah; *b.* sought God in days of Zechariah; *c.* took not away

the high places; *d.* power fatal to him; *e.* smitten with leprosy in the temple; *f.* thrust out by priests to a several house; *g.* Jotham his son regent; *h.* Uzziah's death and burial.

9. *Contemporaneous history:* a. Syria; b. Assyria; c. Edom; d. Philistines and Arabians; e. Ammon; f. Egypt.

10. *Prophets in this section:* I. Judah: a. prophets (to Joash), 2 Chron. xxiv. 19; b. man of God and prophet (to Amaziah), 2 Chron. xxv. 7, 15; c. Zechariah, 2 Chron. xxvi. 5. II. Israel: a. Jonah (to Jeroboam II) 2 Kings xiv. 25.

11. *Contemporaneous literary prophets:* a. Jonah, cf. i. 1, with 2 Kings xiv. 25; b. Hosea i. 1; c. Amos i. 1; d. Isaiah i. 1.

Literature:

Geikie, Hours, vol. iv. chaps. 7 and 9.
Blaikie, Manual, chap. 10, sec. 4; chap. 11, sec. 3.
Edersheim, Bible History, vol. vii. chaps. 4–6.
Stanley, Jewish Church, Lecs. 33 and 37.
Rawlinson, Kings of Israel and Judah, chaps. 20–24.
Old Testament Student, Feb. 1888.
Geikie, Old Testament Characters, on *Jonah, Jeroboam II.*
Smith, Old Test. History, chap. 24.
Farrar, F. W, The Minor Prophets, Men of the Bible Series.

§64. ANARCHY IN ISRAEL. IDOLATRY IN JUDAH.

B. C. 760–728.

Judah—Jotham (16), Ahaz (16).
Israel—Shallum (1 m.), Menahem (10), Pekahiah (2), Pekah (20).

1. *Reign of Shallum of Israel*, 2 Kings xv. 10, 13–15: *a.* usurper, having slain Zechariah; *b.* began 39th year of Uzziah; *c.* slain at end of a month by Menahem.
2. *Reign of Menahem of Israel*, 2 Kings xv. 14, 16–22: *a.* usurper, having slain Shallum; *b.* smote and destroyed Tiphsah; *c.* did evil as Jeroboam; *d.* tributary to Pul (Tiglath-pileser) of Assyria; *e.* exactions from the people; *f.* died.
3. *Reign of Pekahiah (son of Menahem) of Israel*, 2 Kings xv. 22–26: *a.* began in 50th year of Uzziah; *b.* did evil; *c.* slain in his capital at Samaria by Pekah, his captain.
4. *Reign of Pekah of Israel*, 2 Kings xv. 25–31, 37; xvi. 1, 5: *a.* usurper; *b.* began 52d year of Uzziah; *c.* did as Jeroboam; *d.* raid and captives of Tiglath-pileser of Assyria; *e.* league with Rezin of Syria against Ahaz of Judah; *f.* slain by Hoshea in a conspiracy, inspired by Assyria.
5. *Reign of Jotham (son of Uzziah) of Judah*, 2 Kings xv. 5, 32–38; 2 Chron. xxvii: *a.*

regent with Uzziah; *b.* did right as Uzziah, *but* entered not into the temple of Jehovah; *c.* built castles and towers in tops of mountains; *d.* subjugated and subsidized Ammon; *e.* became mighty because, 2 Chron. xxvii. 4–6; *f.* death.

6. *Reign of Ahaz of Judah, politically,* 2 Kings xvi. 1–20; xvii. 13–20; 2 Chron. xxviii; Isaiah vii. 1–20: *a.* began 17th year of Pekah; *b.* delivered to Syria, results; *c.* delivered to Israel with Pekah, results; *d.* 200,000 captives returned at Oded's injunction; *e.* Ahaz appeals to Tiglath-pileser for help; *f.* gifts of treasures; *g.* goes to Damascus to do obeisance to Tiglath-pileser; *h.* raid of Philistines on southeast; *i.* Ahaz's tribute to Assyria.

7. *Reign of Ahaz of Judah, religiously:* *a.* did evil as kings of Israel; *b.* made images of Baalim; *c.* burnt his children in fire to Moloch; *d.* robbed house of Jehovah; *e.* made a Damascus altar; *f.* sacrificed to the gods of Damascus; *g.* shut up house of Jehovah; *h.* put idolatrous altars in every corner of Jerusalem; *i.* did according to the abominations of the heathen whom Jehovah cast out from before the children of Israel; *j.* death and burial.

8. *Contemporaneous history:* *a.* Assyria; *b.* Syria; *c.* Edom; *d.* Egypt.

9. *Kings of Israel and Judah mentioned in Assyrian inscriptions:* a. Uzziah; b. Ahaz; c. Pekah; d. Menahem.

   NOTE—"Land of Omri" is mentioned several times.

10. *Prophets active in this section:* I. Judah: a. Isaiah; b. Micah. II. Israel: a. Amos; b. Oded.

    NOTE—Several unnamed, as in 2 Kings xvii. 13.

Literature:

Geikie, Hours, vol. iv. chaps. 10 and 11.
Blaikie, Manual, chap. 10, sec. 3; chap. 11, sec. 3.
Edersheim, Bible History, vol. vii. chaps. 7 and 8.
Stanley, Jewish Church, Lec. 34 in part.
Rawlinson, Kings of Israel and Judah, chaps. 24–27.
Old Test. Student, March 1888.
Cuneiform Inscriptions and Old Testament, vol. i. pp. 215–257.
Sayce, Fresh Light from Ancient Monuments, chap. 6.
Sayce, The Times of Isaiah.
Driver, S. R., Isaiah, Men of the Bible.
Farrar, Minor Prophets, Men of the Bible.
Expositor's Bible, Isaiah, vol. i.

TENTH PERIOD.

JUDAH ALONE. FALL OF SAMARIA TO FALL OF JERUSALEM.
B. C. 722-587.

§65. { REFORM IN JUDAH.
      { DOWNFALL OF ISRAEL.

Judah—Hezekiah (29).
Israel—Hoshea (9).

1. *Reign of Hoshea of Israel*, 2 Kings xvii. 1–4: *a.* enthroned by Tiglath-pileser (C. O. T. vol. ii. p. 251 sq.); *b.* began in 12th year of Ahaz; *c.* tributary to Shalmaneser; *d.* attempted league with So of Egypt; *e.* imprisonment by Shalmaneser.
2. *Fall of Samaria* (722 B. C.), 2 Kings xvii. 5, 6; xviii. 9–11: *a.* besieged by Shalmaneser of Assyria; *b.* at the end of three years captured by his successor, Sargon; *c.* Sargon's own account of it, made captive 27,280 inhabitants; *d.* put the country under a governor, most of the inhabitants remaining in the land.
3. *Why did Samaria and Israel fall?* 2 Kings xvii. 7–23: *a.* sinned against Jehovah; *b.* served other Gods; *c.* built high places; *d.* set up obelisks and Asherim; *e.* disregarded

seer and prophet; *f.* worshipped host of heaven; *g.* burnt children to heathen gods.

4. *Fate of the captives*, 2 Kings xvii. 6, 23; xviii. 11: *a.* carried to Assyria, Halah, Habor, Gozan; *b.* among the Medes.

5. *Importations into Samaria*, 2 Kings xvii. 24–41; *a.* Assyrian custom of deportation of peoples; *b.* sources of these importations; *c.* their trouble in Samaria; *d.* priest of Jehovah returned to them; *e.* their gods; *f.* their subsequent worship; *g.* their name, Samaritans.

6. *The Samaritans* (see Smith, Bib. Dict.): *a.* their origin; *b.* location; *c.* worship; *d.* later attitude toward the Jews; *e.* Christ's words concerning them; *f.* their later history; *g.* present condition.

7. *Hezekiah's beginning against idolatry*, 2 Kings xviii. 1–8: *a.* did right as David; *b.* removed high places; *c.* brake obelisks; *d.* cut down Asherah; *e.* brake in pieces Moses' serpent.

8. *Hezekiah's reform in the temple service*, 2 Chron. xxix: *a.* opened doors of house of Jehovah; *b.* priests sanctify themselves; *c.* house of Jehovah cleansed and sanctified; *d.* solemn sacrifices with music of David and Asaph; *e.* burnt offerings, priests helped by Levites; *f.* great rejoicing.

9. *Hezekiah's political prosperity:* *a.* rebelled

against Assyria; *b.* conquered Philistines; *c.* in favor with Egypt.
10. *Observance of the passover*, 2 Chron. xxx—xxxi. 1: *a.* its last observance previous to this; *b.* call by letters to all from Dan to Beersheba; *c.* response by Asher, Zebulon and Manasseh; *d.* unclean of Ephraim, Manasseh, Issachar and Zebulon eat the passover (vs. 19); *e.* passover observed fourteen days; *f.* gifts of Hezekiah and princes; *g.* assembly destroys idolatry out of the land.
11. *Provisions for continuous temple worship*, 2 Chron. xxxi. 2–19: *a.* courses of Levites; *b.* the king's portion; *c.* Levite's portion in Jerusalem; *d.* tithes renewed; *e.* surplus provided for.
12. *Hezekiah's great prosperity—why?* 2 Chron. xxxi. 20, 21.
13. *Contemporaneous history:* *a.* Assyria; *b.* Egypt; *c.* Syria; *d.* Phœnicia.
14. *Prophets active at this time:* *a.* Isaiah; *b.* Micah.

Literature:

Geikie, Hours, vol. iv. chaps. 8 and 12.
Blaikie, Manual, chap. 12, sec. 1.
Edersheim, Bible History, vol. vii. chap. 10.
Stanley, Jewish Church, Lec. 38.
Rawlinson, Kings of Israel and Judah, chaps. 28 and 29.
Old Testament Student, March 1888.

Cuneiform Inscriptions and Old Testament vol. i. pp. 251–278.
Sayce, Fresh Light from Ancient Monuments.
" Life and Times of Isaiah.
Driver, Isaiah, Men of the Bible.
Farrar, Minor Prophets, Men of the Bible.
Smith, G. A., Isaiah, vol. i., Expositor's Bible.

§66. HEZEKIAH'S REIGN AFTER FALL OF SAMARIA.

1. *Review causes, siege and capture of Samaria.*
2. *Give the kings (1) of Judah (2) of Israel with length of reigns.*
3. *Sargon's invasion,* 2 Kings xviii. 13; Isa. xx: *a.* for Sennacherib, substitute Sargon in 2 Kings xviii. 13; *b.* Jerusalem not disturbed; *c.* Ashdod and Ethiopians made captives.
4. *Hezekiah's sickness,* 2 Kings xx. 1–11; 2 Chron. xxxii. 24–26; Isa. xxxviii: *a.* before Sennacherib's invasion: (*1*) treasury still full, Isa. xxxix. 2, 6, contrasted with 2 Kings xviii. 14–16; (*2*) deliverance from Assyria still in the future, Isa. xxxviii. 6; (*3*) no reference to deliverance in Hezekiah's psalm of thanksgiving—inexplicable if that were past; (*4*) Sennacherib began to reign, 705 B. C.; (*5*) Hezekiah began to reign, 728 B. C.—3d year of Hoshea of Israel, 2 Kings xviii. 1, sickness about 713 B. C.; *b.* character, inflammatory cutaneous disease or ulcers, Lev. xiii.

8; Ex. ix. 9 sq.; Deut. xxviii. 27; Job. ii. 7; *c.* meaning: (*a*) urge Hezekiah to better works; (*b*) turn him to himself and to his God, Isa. xxxviii. 17; *d.* Isaiah's prophecy, Isa. xxxviii. 1-8; 2 Kings xx. 5, 6; *e.* dial or steps, of Ahaz: (*a*) asking for signs frequent, Judg. vi. 17, 36 sq.; 1 Sam. ii. 34; Matt. xii. 38; xvi. 1, etc.; (*b*) 2 Kings xx. 11, says *shadow*; Isaiah says *shadow with the sun*; (*c*) was it (*1*) refraction, (*2*) eclipse (there was one Sep. 13, 713 B. C.), (*3*) optical illusion, or (*4*) miraculous.

5. *Hezekiah's psalm of thanksgiving*, Isa. xxxviii. 10–20: Analyze this carefully after three attentive readings.

6. *Embassy of M(B)erodach-baladan* (ca. 710 B. C.), 2 Kings xx. 12–19; 2 Chron. xxxii. 31; Isa. xxxix: *a.* who were they? *b.* relations to Assyria; *c.* purpose of embassy: (*1*) congratulations, (*2*) inquire about dial, (*3*) effect a league, (*4*) espionage, (*5*) on God's part, "God left him to try him that he might know all that was in his heart," 2 Chron. xxxii. 31; *d.* reception: (*1*) friendly, (*2*) intimacy established, (*3*) pride exhibited; *e.* result: (*1*) to Hezekiah, (*a*) rebuke by Isaiah, (*b*) captivity foretold, (*c*) God's right recognized; (*2*) to embassy: (*a*) knew Judah and Jerusalem, (*b*) strengthened themselves in the southwest.

7. *Sennacherib's invasion* (701 B. C.), Isa. xiv. 24–27; xxxvi—xxxvii. 10; 2 Kings xviii. 14—chap. xix; 2 Chron. xxxii. 1–23 (cf. Isa. xxii. 1–14; xvii. 12–14; xviii. 1–7): *a.* who was Sennacherib? *b.* object of this expedition; *c.* time of his approach to Palestine, Isa. x; *d.* Hezekiah's water works; *e.* first demands before Jerusalem: (*1*) language spoken, (*2*) arguments for surrender; *f.* second set of messengers to Jerusalem; *g.* Hezekiah's use of the letter; *h.* Judah's relations to Egypt; *i.* Isaiah's protest against alliance, Isa. xviii., xix., xx. 4–6; xxx. 1–7; *j.* Hezekiah's tribute to Sennacherib; *k.* influence on Judah, Isa. xxii; *l.* fate of Assyrian army; *m.* Byron's poem; *n.* Isaiah's prophecy; *o.* death of Sennacherib.
8. *During Hezekiah's whole career, review by events even to details:* *a.* reforms political and religous; *b.* capture of Samaria; *c.* Sargon's invasion; *d.* Hezekiah's sickness; *e.* embassy from Babylon; *f.* Sennacherib's invasion; *g.* Isaiah's prominence in his reign; *h.* Hezekiah's death.
9. *Contemporaneous history*, cf. especially Rawlinson and Old Testament Student: *a.* Assyria; *b.* Babylon; *c.* Syria; *d.* Ethiopia; *e.* Egypt.
10. *Prophets active at this time:* *a.* Isaiah; *b.* Micah.

Literature:

Geikie, Hours, vol. iv. chaps. 13–17, vol. v. 1.

Blaikie, Manual, chap. 11, sec. 4.
Edersheim, Bible History, vol. yii. chaps. 11–13.
Stanley, Jewish Church, Lec. 38 in part.
Rawlinson, Kings of Israel and Judah, chap. 29.
Sayce, Fresh Light from Ancient Monuments.
" Life and Times of Isaiah.
Cuneiform Inscriptions and Old Testament, vol. i. p. 278—vol. ii. p. 39.
Driver, Isaiah, Men of the Bible.
Farrar, Minor Prophets, Men of the Bible.
Smith, G. A., Isaiah, vol. i., Expositor's Bible.
Old Test. Student, March 1888.
Smith, O. T. History, chap. 25 in part.

§67. REIGNS OF MANASSEH (55) AND AMON (2).
B. C. ca. 698–641.

2 Kings xxi; 2 Chron. xxxiii.

1. *Condition of Judah at the close of Hezekiah's reign:* a. religiously; b. politically.
2. *Accession of Manasseh:* a. at twelve years of age; b. had a righteous father, and probably a righteous mother; c. but evil counsellors.
3. *Reasons for an anti-religious movement:* a. supremacy of Jehovah worship since Ahaz's time; b. presence of idolaters in the court; c. presence of foreigners in the land; d. seeming scarcity of prophets and faithful priests.

4. *Kinds of heathen worship revived and introduced, describe each:* a. high places; b. Baal; c. Asherah; d. all the host of heaven; e. burnt his children in fire, see §24. 8; f. practiced augury and enchantments.

NOTE. — Valley of Hinnom-Tophet, Jer. vii. 31, 32; Ezek. xxiii. 37, 39.

5. *Manasseh's persecutions of the faithful:* a. shed innocent blood, very much, 2 Kings xxi. 4; b. traditional death of Isaiah; c. cf. Jezebel and Athaliah's persecutions — conflicts between idolatry and true worship.

6. *Jehovah's prophets and words to Manasseh*, 2 Kings xxi. 10–16; 2 Chron. xxxiii. 10: a. some prophets still alive; b. Jerusalem to be as Samaria; c. remnant to be delivered into the hands of spoilers.

7. *Manasseh's captivity*, 2 Chron. xxxiii. 11–13; a. Judah in league with S. W. peoples against Assyria; b. Asurbanipal, king of Assyria and Babylon, captures Manasseh; c. penitence; d. return; e. occurred about 672 B.C.

8. *Manasseh's reform and death:* a. attempts to undo his former wicked deeds; b. but only of a superficial nature; c. death and burial.

9. *Amon's reign*, 2 Kings xxi. 19–26; 2 Chron. xxxiii. 21–25; a. "Amon" is the name of an Egyptian deity; b. began at 22 years of age; c. did evil as Manasseh; d. served images Manasseh had made; e. slain by his servants in his own house; f. buried in his own sepulchre.

1

10. *Contemporaneous history:* a. Assyria; b. Babylon; c. Egypt.
11. *Prophets active:* a. 2 Kings xxi. 10; b. 2 Chron. xxxiii. 10; c. 2 Chron. xxxiii. 18.

Literature:

Geikie, Hours, vol. v. chaps. 2–4.
Blaikie, Manual, chap. 11, sec. 4.
Edersheim, Bible History, vol. vii. chap. 14.
Stanley, Jewish Church, Lec. 39.
Rawlinson, Kings of Israel and Judah, chaps. 30, 31.
Sayce, Fresh Light from Ancient Monuments.
Cun. Inscrip. and Old Test., vol. ii. pp. 39–43.
Old Test. Student, May 1888.
Smith, Old Test. History, chap. 25.

§68. JOSIAH'S REIGN AND REFORMS.

B. C. 641–610.

2 Kings xxii—xxiii. 30; 2 Chron. xxxiv., xxxv; Jer. i—x; Zeph. i—iii. and Nahum.

1. *Accession of Josiah:* a. at eight years of age; b. walked in ways of David his father.
2. *Condition of Judah at beginning of Josiah's reign:* a. politically; b. religiously.
3. *Reasons for a revival:* a. the pendulum must swing back; b. Josiah's early training; c. faithful few; d. preaching of the prophets; e. probably a Scythian invasion.

4. *Josiah's purifications in and out of Jerusalem:*
   a. of idols: (*1*) Asherah in the temple, (*2*) Baal vessels, etc., (*3*) graven and molten images of all kinds, (*4*) sun images, (*5*) horses and chariots of the sun; *b.* places of worship: (*1*) high places, (*2*) Tophet, (*3*) houses of Sodomites, (*4*) altars of Ahaz on housetops, (*5*) altars of Manasseh in courts of house of Jehovah, (*6*) high places of Solomon, (*7*) altar of Jeroboam son of Nebat at Bethel, (*8*) high places in Samaria, Simeon and Naphtali; *c.* worshippers: (*1*) put down idolatrous priests at Jerusalem, (*2*) sacrificed the priests on the altars, (*3*) burned priests' bones on the altar, (*4*) remarkable fulfillment of prophecy, 2 Kings xxiii. 16, with 1 Kings xiii. 2 (345 years earlier).

5. *Repairs of the temple and discovery of the law:*
   a. collections inside and outside of Jerusalem; *b.* repairs of wood and stone; *c.* scroll of law found—that it had existed at an earlier day is shown: (*1*) by its instant recognition, (*2*) by its briefness, as only Deuteronomy could have been read through in one session, (*3*) at coronation of Joash, the testimony was put into his hands, (*4*) David directed services according to the law of Jehovah, (*5*) Joshua read the law at Gerizim; *d.* in 18th year of his reign.

6. *Effect of this "find" on king and people:* a. at its reading Josiah rends his clothes; b. Huldah, the prophetess, inquires of Jehovah for him; c. people assembled; d. law read; e. covenant entered into.
7. *Re-institution of the passover:* a. exactly in accordance with the law; b. more complete than since the judges; c. further cleansing of the land of witches, etc.
8. *Real condition of Judah as a people:* Jer. i—x.
9. *Relations of Egypt to the East, Nineveh and Babylon.*
10. *Josiah's rashness and death:* a. Necho's expedition; b. Josiah's eastern lord, who was he? c. Josiah rebuked; d. rashness and death; e. elegy of Jeremiah and mourning of all Israel.
11. *Josiah's character and work:* a. intensely religious; b. poor politician; c. medium force; d. work necessarily superficial; e. not always wise.
12. *Contemporaneous history:* a. Assyria; b. Babylon; c. Egypt.
13. *Prophets active now:* a. Huldah; b. Jeremiah; c. Nahum; d. Zephaniah.

Literature:

Geikie, Hours, vol. v. chaps. 5, 8–11.
Blaikie, Manual, chap. 11. sec. 4.
Edersheim, Bible History, vol. vii. chaps. **15 and 16**.
Stanley, Jewish Church, Lec. 39 in part.

Rawlinson, Kings of Israel and Judah, chap. 32.
Cun. Inscrip. and Old Testament, vol. ii. pp. 43–47.
Old Test. Student, May 1888.
Geikie, Old Test. Characters, on *Josiah*.
Cheyne, T. K., Jeremiah, Men of the Bible.
Smith, Old Test. History, chap. 25 in part.
Farrar, Minor Prophets, Men of the Bible.
Ball, C. J., Jeremiah, Expositor's Bible.

§69. DECLINE UNDER JEHOAHAZ (3 M.) AND JEHOIAKIM (11).

B. C. 609–599.

2 Kings xxiii. 30—xxiv. 6; 2 Chron. xxxvi. 1–8; Jer. xxii. 18, 19; xxv., xxvi., xxvii. 1–11; xxxv., xxxvi., xlv., xlvi. 1–12; xlvii.

1. *Give the kings of Judah in order, with length of reigns.*
2. *Condition of Judah at accession of Jehoahaz.*
3. *Career of Jehoahaz;* 2 Kings xxiii. 30–34; 2 Chron. xxxvi. 1–4; Jer. xxii. 11, 12: *a.* made king by the people; *b.* deposed after three months by Necho; *c.* land taxed; *d.* Jehoahaz exiled in Egypt.
4. *Jehoiakim's accession:* *a.* set up by Necho as his subject; *b.* name changed from Eliakim; *c.* tribute paid to Egypt.
5. *Jeremiah's deliverance to Jehoiakim,* xxvi., xxvii.

1–11: *a.* captivity of Judah; *b.* fall of Jerusalem; *c.* overthrow of Babylon; *d.* fall of all the nations of the East, all on account of sins of Judah.
6. *Jehoiakim's religious policy:* *a.* suppression of the prophets: (*1*) Urijah, (*2*) Jeremiah, (*3*) 2 Kings xxiv. 4; *b.* destruction of prophecies against himself: (*1*) events leading to the reading of the roll, (*2*) cutting and burning the same, (*3*) hunt for the originators.
7. *Contemporaneous history:* *a.* Assyria; *b.* Babylon; *c.* Egypt; *d.* Syria.
8. *Give a full statement regarding the geographical points in this section.*
9. *Prophets active here:* *a.* Jeremiah; *b.* Urijah; *c.* Zephaniah; *d.* Habakkuk.

Literature:

Geikie, Hours, vol. v. chaps. 13–15.
Blaikie, Manual, chap. 11, sec. 5.
Edersheim, Bible History, vol. vii. chaps. 16 and 17.
Stanley, Jewish Church, Lec. 40.
Rawlinson, Kings of Israel and Judah, chap. 33.
Old Test. Student, June 1888.
Geikie, Old Test. Characters, on *Jehoiakim.*
Cheyne, Jeremiah, Men of the Bible.
Sayce, Fresh Lights from Ancient Monuments.
Farrar, Minor Prophets, Men of the Bible.
Ball, Jeremiah, Expositor's Bible.
Smith, Old Test. History, chap. 25 in part.

§70. FINAL DECLINE UNDER JEHOIACHIN (3 M.) AND ZEDEKIAH (11). B. C. 699—587.

I. *Jehoiachin*, 2 Kings xxiv. 8-16; xxv. 27-30; 2 Chron. xxxvi. 9, 10; Jer. xxii. 20-30; xxiv. 1; xxix.

1. *Political status of Judah:* a. subject to Babylon; b. probably suspecting revolt, Nebukadrezzar lays siege to Jerusalem; c. king, princes, artizans, come out and surrender; d. carried to Babylon.
2. *Religious policy of Jehoiachin:* a. did evil in the sight of Jehovah; b. provoked Jeremiah, who called him a " despised broken vessel" (xxvi. 28); c. brought on his captivity.
3. *Jeremiah's attitude:* a. Jer. xiii. 18-21; b. xxii. 24-30.

II. *Zedekiah*, 2 Kings xxiv. 17—xxv. 7; 2 Chron. xxxvi. 11-16; Jer. xxi. 1-10; xxii; xxvii. 12-22; xxviii., xxxii—xxxiv., xxxvii—xxxix; lii. 1-11.

1. *Accession:* a. *third* son of Josiah; b. began 598 B. C.; c. Mattaniah (gift of Jah) changed to Zedekiah (righteousness of Jah), cf. Jer. xxiii. 5, 6; d. vassal to Babylon.
2. *Religious policy of Zedekiah:* a. at first, favorable to law of Moses: (*1*) declaring freedom to Jewish slaves under Jewish masters, (*2*) sending exhortations to captives at Babylon.

i

3. *Embassies to Babylon:* *a.* with Jeremiah's letter, Jer. xxix. 1–20; *b.* Zedekiah's trip to Babylon, Jer. li. 59–64: (*1*) to relieve suspicions, (*2*) to re-affirm allegiance to Babylon.
4. *Political entanglements with Egypt:* *a.* advice of the Egyptian party; *b.* new king, Hophra, on throne of Egypt; *c.* false prophecies about early fall of Babylon, Jer. xxviii. 1–11; *d.* petty kings who were ambassadors to Jerusalem, Jer. xxvii. 3; *e.* Zedekiah sent ambassadors to Egypt to negotiate an alliance, Ezek. xvii. 5; *f.* league with Egypt probably made; *g.* open rebellion against Babylon, 2 Kings xxiv. 20; 2 Chron. xxxvi. 13 (589 B. C.).
5. *Jeremiah's zeal against Zedekiah's decision:* *a.* avoid Egypt; *b.* be faithful to Babylon; *c.* serve Jehovah.
6. *Approach of the Babylonian army:* *a.* the army with Nebukadrezzar in person; *b.* recourse to divination, Ezek. xxi. 20–22; *c.* ravaging of Judah; *d.* encampment about Jerusalem.
7. *Contemporaneous history:* *a.* Babylon; *b.* Egypt; *c.* Media.
8. *Prophets active now:* *a.* Jeremiah; *b.* 2 Chron. xxxvi. 16.

Literature:

Geikie, Hours, vol. v. chaps. 17 and 18.
Blaikie, Manual, chap. 11, secs. 5 and 6.

Edersheim, Bible History, vol. vii. chap. 17.
Stanley, Jewish Church, Lec. 40 in part.
Rawlinson, Kings of Israel and Judah, chap. 34.
Cun. Inscrip. and Old Testament, vol. ii. pp. 37–42.
Cheyne, Jeremiah, His Life and Times.
Ball, Jeremiah, Expositor's Bible.
Farrar, Minor Prophets, Men of the Bible.
Geikie, O. T. Characters, on *Jeremiah*.
Old Test. Student, June 1888.
Smith, Old Test. History, chap. 25.

1

ELEVENTH PERIOD.

EXILE. FALL OF JERUSALEM TO FALL OF BABYLON. B. C. 587—537.

§71. THE FALL OF JERUSALEM. 587 B. C.

Jer. xxv. 8–38; xxi. 1—xxii. 1–9; xxiv., xxxii., xxxiii., xxxiv; 2 Kings xxv. 8–22; 2 Chron. xxxvi. 17–21; Jer. lii. 12–30; Jer. xxxix., xl.

1. *Its prediction, when and by whom?* *a.* Isaiah to Hezekiah, 2 Kings xx. 17; *b.* prophets to Manasseh, 2 Kings xxi. 10–16; *c.* Huldah to Josiah, 2 Kings xxii. 16, 17, with Deut. xxviii. 25, 52–68; *d.* Jeremiah to Jehoiakim, Jer. xxv. 9–11; *e.* Jeremiah to Zedekiah, Jer. xxxiv. 2, 3; of the minor prophets, Micah iii. 12; vii. 13; Zephaniah i. 2–6.

2. *Mediate and immediate causes:* I. mediate: *a.* alliances between Solomon and outside peoples; *b.* between Jehoshaphat and Ahab; *c.* corruption of kings of Judah; *d.* rebellion of kings of Judah against their masters. II. immediate: *a.* entanglements with Egypt; *b.* Zedekiah's rebellion against Babylon; *c.* his disregard of Jeremiah and all the prophets; *d.* his obstinacy at the siege.

3. *The investment:* a. location of the city; b. camp of Babylonians; c. methods of siege; d. time.
4. *Occurrences during the siege:* a. consternation of the people; b. exhortations of prophets; c. interposition of Egypt; d. threatened famine; e. attempted negotiations; f. plans of escape.
5. *Jeremiah's personal attitude:* a. advises surrender, submission; b. sides with chastisers.
6. *Capture and plunderings, at end of eighteen months:* a. breach made in the walls; b. flight of king and army; c. capture of king and attendants; d. carrying off the population.
7. *Treatment of the captives:* a. Zedekiah condemned at Riblah; b. his sons and princes slain before him; c. his own eyes put out; d. sent in fetters to Babylon.
8. *Treatment of Jeremiah.*
9. *Nebuzaradan's return and destruction of Jerusalem:* a. plunderings; b. fire; c. razing the walls; d. carrying away the people.
10. Review the five captivities of Jerusalem by *Nebukadrezzar*, cf. Jer. lii. 28-30.
11. *Significance of the fall of Jerusalem for Judah:* a. end of city of David; b. end of the nation; c. end of the temple-centre of Jehovah worship; d. end of a home for Israel.

Literature:

Geikie, Hours, vol. vi. chaps. 3-6.
Blaikie, Manual, chap. 12, sec. 1.

THE EXILE. 147

Stanley, Jewish Church, Lec. 40.
Rawlinson, Kings of Israel and Judah, chap. 34.
Cun. Inscrip. and Old Testament, vol. ii. pp. 47–51.
Cheyne, Jeremiah, His Life and Times.
Ball, Jeremiah, Expositor's Bible.
Old Test. Student, June 1888.
Smith, Old Test. History, chap. 26.
Price, Syllabus of the Minor Prophets, pp. 13, 15.

§72. REMNANTS IN PALESTINE AND EGYPT.

2 Kings xxv. 22–26; Jer. xl–xliv; Ezek. xxxvi.

1. *Provisions of Nebukadrezzar for the remnant in Palestine:* a. Gedaliah appointed governor by Nebukadrezzar over all remaining in the cities and in the country; b. his exhortations to the people; c. return of the Jews out of Moab, Ammon and Edom.
2. *Murder of Gedaliah by Ishmael of seed royal:* a. Gedaliah warned by Johanan; b. Gedaliah, Jews and Chaldeans smitten at Mizpah; c. Ishmael slays seventy men from Shechem; d. ten from Shechem saved; e. leads captive the house of Gedaliah.
3. *Johanan's supremacy:* a. Johanan's pursuit of Ishmael; b. Ishmael's flight and return of captives; c. Johanan's victory, and home near Bethlehem.

4. *Jeremiah's word of-Jehovah to this remnant:* a. be content here and Jehovah will build you up; b. enter Egypt and ye shall die by sword, pestilence and famine.
5. *Their flight into Egypt:* a. against Jeremiah's warnings they go down to Egypt; b. Jeremiah and Baruch taken along; c. other Jews there, Jer. xxiv. 8, 9; xliv. 1.
6. *Jeremiah's prophecy at Tahpahnes:* a. announcing Nebukadrezzar's supremacy there; b. destruction of Egypt's gods; c. destruction of the Jews on account of their wickedness.
7. *Social and literary surroundings of the Jews in Egypt:* a. abundant wealth; b. luxury on all hands; c. vice regnant; d. idolatry everywhere; e. women's replies to Jeremiah.
8. *End of the Jewish exiles in Egypt:* a. perished there for the most part; b. a few returned to Judah, Jer. xliv. 14, 27; c. some were carried to Babylon (Josephus).
9. *Political history of Egypt during the exile of these Jews.*
10. *Ezekiel's prophecies concerning the fate of Egypt.* Chaps. xxix. 17–21; xxx., xxxii.
11. *Condition of Palestine during the remaining years of the Babylonian exile.*
12. *Means of intercommunication between the exiled Jews of various countries.*

1

THE EXILE. 149

Literature:

Geikie, Hours, vol. vi. chaps. 9 and 10.
Stanley, Jewish Church, Lec. 40 in part.
Old Test. Student, June 1888.
Cheyne, Jeremiah, His Life and Times.
Ball, The Prophecies of Jeremiah, Expositor's Bible.
Smith, Old Test. History, chap. 26 in part.

§73. THE BABYLONIAN EXILE OF THE JEWS.

Ezek. iii., xi. 14-25; xii. 21-28; xiv., xvii—xx., xxxiii., xxxiv; Jer. xxix; Dan. i., ii.

1. *Its prediction, when and by whom?* a. Isaiah to Hezekiah, 2 Kings xx. 17, 18; b. Micah to Judah, iv. 10; c. Jeremiah, xxv. 11; xxxiv. 2, 3.
2. *Captivities initiating this exile—all by Nebukadrezzar:* a. third year of Jehoiakim, (ca. 607 B. C.), 2 Kings xxiv. 1; 2 Chron. xxxvi. 6, 7; Dan. i. 1, 2; b. close of Jehoiakim's reign, (ca. 599 B. C.), Jer. lii. 28, 3,023 persons; c. beginning of Jehoiachin's reign, (ca. 598 B. C.), 2 Kings xxiv. 10-16; 2 Chron. xxxvi. 10, 10,000 persons; d. double deportation at fall of Jerusalem, (*1*) 2 Kings xxv. 8-21; 2 Chron. xxxvi. 18-20; Jer. xxxix. 8-10; lii. 12-27, (*2*) Jer. lii. 29, 832 persons; e. deportation of a remnant, Jer. lii. 30, 745 persons, (ca. 583 B. C.)

3. *Babylonian empire:* *a.* extent; *b.* capital; *c.* king; *d.* political policy; *e.* religious policy; *f.* history.
4. *Localities assigned to the exiles:* *a.* in Babylon, *e.g.* Daniel and companions; *b.* on the Chebar, *e. g.* Ezekiel; *c.* among all the peoples of the empire, Jer. xxix. 14, 7; iii. 18, and often.
5. *Classes of exiles:* *a.* those in favor with the court, Dan. i. 19–21; ii. 46–49; *b.* common laborers — lower classes, Jer. xxix; Ezek. xiii; *c.* pretentious prophets, Ezek. xiii; Jer. xxix.
6. *Social condition of the exiles:* *a.* Jehoiachin, 2 Kings xxv. 27, and Daniel, i. 19–21, etc.; *b.* others ill treated, cf. Isa. lx. 1; *c.* well treated, cf. Jer. xxix. 4–7; also Ezek. and Esther throughout; *d.* maintained family and tribal relations.
7. *Political condition of the exiles:* *a.* subjects of Babylon; *b.* with longing for Jerusalem; *c.* other points?
8. *Religious condition of the exiles,* cf. Geikie, vi. 16: *a.* idolatry rampant, cf. Ezek. viii; Jer. xliv; *b.* false prophets active, Jer. xxix. 4–8; *c.* Ezekiel faithful to Jehovah; *d.* a few followers cling to the true faith; *e.* other points?
9. *Institutions during the exile:* *a.* fasts, Zech. vii. 2, 3, 5; *b.* schools, Ezra viii. 15–20.
10. *Literary activity in the exile:* *a.* Jeremiah's

later prophecies, given in Egypt; *b.* Ezekiel's (595–572 B. C.) wonderfully logical and forcible prophecies; *c.* Ezra's collection and editing of texts; *d.* establishment of schools, formulating of lengthy traditions, etc.

11. *Daniel in Babylon:* *a.* trained in the court; *b.* employed in the court; *c.* interprets Nebukadrezzar's dream, Dan. i. 16–21; ii. 1–49.

12. *Contemporaneous history of Babylon.*

Literature:

Geikie, Hours, vol. v. chap. 20; vi. chaps. 11 and 13.
Blaikie, Manual, chap. 12. secs. 3 and 4.
Stanley, Jewish Church, Lec. 41.
Daniel, His Life and Times, Men of the Bible.
Cun. Inscrip. and Old Test. vol. ii. pp. 124–136.
Old and New Test. Student, July and Aug. 1889.
Smith, Old Test. History, chap. 26.

TWELFTH PERIOD.

THE RETURN. FALL OF BABYLON TO CLOSE OF OLD TESTAMENT.

§74. THE FALL OF BABYLON.
B. C. 537.

1. *Its prediction, by whom and when?* a. Isaiah, chaps. xiii., xiv; xxi. 9, 10; xli. 1-7, etc.; b. Jeremiah, xxv. 12; xxviii. 4, 11; l., li; c. Ezekiel, xxxvii. 15; xxxiv. 39.
2. *Its location, size, importance.*
3. *Kings of Babylon since Nebukadrezzar:* a. names; b. right to the throne; c. character and length of reign; d. chief events of each reign.
4. *Rise of the Persian and Elamite powers:* a. Cyrus' ancestry; b. his first conquests in the East; c. his advances to the North.
5. *Cyrus' conquests in the West:* a. extent; b. methods; c. kind of sovereignty established.
6. *Cyrus' conquests in the region of Babylon:* a. reason of approach; b. policy; c. success.
7. *Belshazzar's feast:* a. king at this time; b. Belshazzar's office; c. kind of feast; d. doings of the banqueters; e. writing on the wall; f. Daniel.

1

8. *Capture of Babylon:* a. last point to be taken; b. easy entrance and capture; c. Daniel's position.
9. *Significance to civilization:* a. end of Semitic sway and Oriental history; b. beginning of classical history; c. beginning of religious liberty; d. emancipation of Jewish exiles.

Literature:

Geikie, Hours, vol. vi. chap. (12, 14, 15 on the prophets) 16.
Blaikie, Manual, chap. 12. sec. 5.
Stanley, Jewish Church, Lec. 42.
Daniel, His Life and Times, Men of the Bible.
Old and New Test. Student, July and Aug. 1889.
Transactions of Society of Biblical Archæology, vol. vii. pp. 139-176.
Smith, Old Test. History, chap. 26.

§75. THE FIRST RETURN.
B. C. 536.

Chron. xxxvi. 22, 23; Ezra i—iii; cf. Pss. xcvii. xcix., cxv., cxxvi.

1. *Edict of Cyrus:* a. substance of it; b. motive in Cyrus' mind; c. Cyrus a monotheist or polytheist? d. political significance.
2. *Assistance given the pilgrims:* a. by command of Cyrus; b. only freewill offerings; c. vessels of the old temple at Jerusalem — 5,400 in number.

3. *Classes of those who returned:* a. 42,360 Jews; b. 7,337 slaves—200 of them singers; c. of 24 courses of priests, four returned, consisting of 4,000 persons; d. 74 Levites.
   NOTE—Were there representatives of *all* the tribes?
4. *The caravan:* a. accompanied by 1000 cavalry, according to tradition; c. four months on the way.
5. *Spirit of the return;* cf. Isa. xl., xlviii. 20, 21; Dan. ix. 20; Ps. cxxxvii: a. religious impulse; b. national pride; c. local attractions—Jerusalem.
6. *Possessors of Palestine at their arrival:* a. under Persian rule; b. occupied by some Jews; c. Samaritan peoples.
7. *Zerubbabel's leadership:* a. ancestry; b. zeal; c. power as leader; d. religious character.
8. *Steps toward rebuilding the temple:* a. collections; b. arrangements with Tyre for timber; c. unanimity of interest.
9. *Re-institution of the rites of worship*, Ps. cxv.
10. *Laying of the corner-stone of the second temple*, Ps. lxxxvii., cvi., cvii., cxviii., cxx–cxxxiv., cxxxvi: a. Levites' part in it; b. joy of young men, sorrow of old men.

Literature:

Geikie, Hours, vol. vi. chap. 17.
Blaikie, Manual, chap. 13, secs. 1 and 2.
Stanley, Jewish Church, Lec. 43, first half.
Old and New Test. Student, Sept. 1890.
Smith, Old Test. History, chap. 27.

§76. BUILDING OF THE SECOND TEMPLE.

Ezra iv—vi; Haggai and Zechariah.

1. *Delay of fifteen years, caused by the Samaritans:* a. ground of opposition; b. means of stopping the work.
2. *Condition of the colony at end of fifteen years:* a. small crops, frequent droughts; b. living in ceiled houses, neglectful of house of Jehovah.
3. *Haggai's work in changing the order of affairs:* a. rebuked the people; b. encouraged them to build the temple; c. gave promise of greater glory here than in the first temple; d. character of Haggai's book.
4. *Cyrus' edict renewed by Darius II:* a. letter to Darius; b. edict of Cyrus found in the records; c. re-issued and Jews strengthened by help of the governor; d. time of this event.
5. *Zechariah's work in urging on the building of the temple:* a. affirms a new beginning; b. foretells great success and glory; c. does it mainly by visions; d. character of Zechariah's book.
6. *Finishing the second temple:* a. time, Ezra vi. 15; b. joy at the dedication; c. extensive sacrifices; d. as written in the book of Moses.
7. *Contemporaneous Persian history,* 537–515 B C.: a. Cyrus, 558–529; b. Cambyses, 529–522;

c. false Smerdis, 8 or 9 months; *d.* Darius (II.) Hystaspes, 521–486.

8. *Other contemporaneous history:* *a.* battle of Marathon, 490 B. C.

Literature:

Geikie, Hours, vol. vi. 17 in part, and 18.
Stanley, Jewish Church, Lec. 43, second half.
Wright, Zechariah and his Prophecies.
Haggai and Zechariah, Cambridge Bible.
Farrar, Minor Prophets, Men of the Bible.
Dods, in The Expositor, 1886.
Old and New Test. Student, Sept. 1889.
Price, Syllabus of the Minor Prophets, pp. 18, 19.
Smith, Old Test. History, chap. 27.

§77. QUEEN ESTHER.

Esther i–x.

1. *Authorship:* Give various views.
2. *Time and place of composition:* *a.* about 478 B. C.; *b.* in Susa — these answers are only probable.
3. *Persian empire:* *a.* extent; *b.* power; *c.* capital; *d.* contemporaneous history.
4. *Susa:* *a.* location; *b.* size; *c.* as excavated to-day.
5. *Special festival in session:* *a.* time of year; *b.* guests; *c.* sumptuousness; *d.* length; *e.* object.
6. *Events leading to the choice of Esther as queen: a.*

banquet of servants; *b.* king's demand of Vashti; *c.* her refusal and deposition; *d.* gathering of maidens; *e.* choice of Esther; *f.* Mordecai's scheme.
7. *Haman's hatred of Jews and edict against them:* *a.* cause; *b.* means of revenge; *c.* distribution and number of Jews in the empire; *d.* effect of this edict on them.
8. *Mordecai's scheme and victory:* *a.* Esther's intercession; *b.* Mordecai's promotion; *c.* Haman's death; *d.* conflict of the Jews; *e.* commemoration of the event — Purim.
9. *Esther as a plot or play.*
10. *Object of this book:* *a.* give an insight into the distribution and power of the Jews at that time; *b.* describe the origin of the feast of Purim.

Literature:

Geikie, Hours, vol. vi. chap. 19.
Blaikie, Manual, chap. 13, sec. 3.
Stanley, Jewish Church, Lec. 45 in part.
Old and New Test. Student., Oct. 1889.
Book of Esther and Palace of Ahasuerus, Bibliotheca Sacra, Oct. 1889.
Geikie, Old Test. Characters, on *Esther.*

§78. SECOND RETURN.—UNDER EZRA.

Ezra vii—x.

1. *Persian history from completion of the second*

temple to Ezra, 517–458 B. C.: *a.* Darius II, 521–486; *b.* Xerxes, 486–465; *c.* Artaxerxes, 465–425.
2. *Preliminary preparations for a journey to Jerusalem:* *a.* decree of Artaxerxes; *b.* assembling at the river Ahava; *c.* search for Levites; *d.* fast; *e.* amount of precious metal; *f.* prepared for the journey.
3. *Journey and arrival:* *a.* time on the way; *b.* safety under way; *c.* arrival and rest; *d.* offerings; *e.* commissions delivered to Persian officers.
4. *Ezra's sorrow and prayer:* *a.* trespass in case of mixed marriages; *b.* Ezra's grief; *c.* substance of Ezra's prayer.
5. *Ezra's victory:* *a.* assembly of people; *b.* oath to put away strange wives and children; *c.* penalty for the one who should disregard this; *d.* time needed for the divorcement cases.

Literature:
Geikie, Hours, vol. vi. chap. 20 in part.
Blaikie, Manual, chap. 13, sec. 4.
Stanley, Jewish Church, Lec. 44 in part.
Old and New Test. Student, Oct.—Dec. 1889.

§79. THE THIRD RETURN.— NEHEMIAH.

Nehemiah i — xiii. Other Scripture same as §78.

1. *Nehemiah at Susa:* *a.* his position; *b.* relation to Mordecai; *c.* influence with the king; *d.*

THE RETURN. 159

means of bringing about his permission to go to Jerusalem.

2. *Return and attendants:* *a.* accompanied by cavalry; *b.* brought letters to governors in the west; *c.* enemies of Israel grieved.
3. *Walls of Jerusalem:* *a.* explored by night; *b.* scorn of Sanballat and company; *c.* orderly building of the walls and gates; *d.* completed in fifty-two days; *e.* dedication, chap. xii. 27 sq.
4. *Opposition of Sanballat and company:* *a.* men of Israel watch and pray; *b.* half-armed for work, half for fight; *c.* builders armed for defense; *d.* people relieved for work by abolishing usury and restoring mortgaged property.
5. *Sanballat's provocation:* *a.* challenge to Nehemiah; *b.* the latter's wise retort; *c.* attempted intimidation of Nehemiah; *d.* challenge to meet in the temple.
6. *Reforms of Ezra and Nehemiah:* *a.* regular reading of the law of Moses; *b.* dwelling in booths at the great feasts; *c.* observance of the Sabbath; *d.* regular service of the temple
7. *Prayer of praise,* chap. 9: analyze it.
8. *Nehemiah's return to Susa, and second journey to Jerusalem:* *a* Tobiah's offence; *b.* appointment of new officers; *c.* Sabbath breaking; *d.* mixed marriages.

9. *Other work of Ezra and Nehemiah:* *a.* collecting sacred books; *b.* interpreting sacred books; *c.* teaching students of the law; *d.* originating synagogue worship.

NOTE.—Idolatry not discoverable after the exile.

Literature:

Geikie, Hours, vol. vi. chap. 20.
Blaikie, Manual, chap. 13, sec. 5.
Stanley, Jewish Church, Lec. 44.
Old and New Testament Student, Jan., Feb. 1890.
Geikie, Old Test. Characters, on *Nehemiah*.

§80. GENERAL REVIEW.

1. Describe the Old Testament world.

2. Describe Palestine in detail.

3. Give the kinds of Literature, the Books, and the number of chapters in each book, in the Old Testament.

4. Give the twelve periods of Old Testament History, with their dates.

5. Give the sections in the first two periods — the introduction to the history of Israel.

6. Give the sections in the next three periods — finishing the Pentateuch.

7. Give the sections in the periods of the Conquest and Judges.

8. Give the sections in the period of the Kingdom.

9. Give the sections in the Dual Kingdom period.

10. Give the sections in the period of Judah Alone.

11. Give the sections in the last two periods of Old Testament History.

12. Try to *think* through each period, naming to yourself each section from beginning to end.

APPENDIX.

THE CHRONOLOGY OF JUDAH AND ISRAEL.

The uncertainty of all early Old Testament chronology renders it unnecessary to begin farther back than the division of the kingdom. The dates of Archbishop Ussher, as given in the Authorized Version, are in the main employed, but FOR CONVENIENCE SAKE ONLY. No revision of these computations has had general acceptance, though their inaccuracy in many cases has been well established. The appended table is intended merely to aid in fixing the synchronism of the kings in the different kingdoms. The date in the first column is a revision and one which is adopted by some scholars for the period from the division of the kingdom to the fall of Samaria. The discrepancies between these two systems will be readily observed, but no attempt will be made in this appendix to harmonize them.

SECTION I.—THE DUAL KINGDOM.

New Date.	Old Date.	JUDAH.	Prophets.	ISRAEL.	Prophets.	Contemporaneous.
938	975	1. Rehoboam (17).	Shemaiah. Iddo.	1. Jeroboam (22). Calf idolatry established at Bethel and Dan.	Ahijah. Man of God.	Shishak of Egypt. Rezon of Syria.
934	970	Invasion of Shishak. Plunder of Jerusalem.		18th year.		
921	957	2. Abijah (3). Defeats Jeroboam.				
918	955	3. Asa (41).		2. Nadab (2), son of Jeroboam I, did evil. Slain by	Iddo.	
917	954	2d year. Reforms.		3. Baasha (24).		
916	953	3d year. Purifies Jerusalem.				
	941	Defeats Zerah. Buys off and combines with Ben-hadad of Syria against Baasha.	Azariah. Hanani.	Builds Ramah against Asa. Invaded by Syria.		Ramman–nirari II of Assyria. Zerah the Ethiopian.
	940					
893	930	26th year.	Jehu.	4. Elah (2). Slain in a drunken row in Tirzah.	Jehu.	

162

B.C. (Judah)	B.C. (Israel)	Judah	Prophets (Judah)	Israel	Prophets (Israel)	Contemporaries
892	929	27th year.		5. Zimri (7 days). 6. (Tibni and) Omri (12). Contest 4 years. Builds Samaria. 7. Ahab (22), married Jezebel of Zidon.		
878	918	38th year. Forgets God. Died and buried in Jerusalem.		4th year. Baal worship planted in Israel.		
	914	4. Jehoshaphat (25). Reforms, political and religious. Subdues Moab and the Philistines.	Jehu.	Famine. Ahab confronts Elijah. Test at Carmel. War with Syria. Naboth's vineyard. War with Syria continued. Death of Ahab.	Elijah, "the prophet," 1 Kings xx. 22. Micaiah.	Ben-hadad II of Syria, 1 Kings xx. 26.
	901			8. Ahaziah (2). Inquires of Baal-zebub.		
856	897	17th year. Alliance with Ahab. Battle at Ramoth Gilead. 18th year. Defeats Ammon and Moab at Engedi. Naval scheme. Jehoram regent with his father.	Jahaziel. Eliezer.	9. Jehoram (12). Combines with Jehoshaphat against Mesha. Besieged in Samaria by Ben-hadad, but relieved.	Elisha.	Mesha king of Moab.
852	896	5. Jehoram (8) alone. Slays his brethren. Jerusalem plundered by Arabs and Philistines. Jehoram dies of sore disease.		11th year. 12th year.		Ben-hadad II of Syria.
844	889	6. Ahaziah (1). Follows house of Ahab.				Hazael of Syria.
843	885	(0). Athaliah (6) usurps the throne. Destroys royal seed except Joash.	Obadiah.	10. Jehu (28). Exterminates house of Ahab and Baal worshippers.		Shalmaneser II of Assyria (869–825)
	884					

New Date.	Old Date.	JUDAH.	Prophets.	ISRAEL.	Prophets.	Contemporaneous.
837	878	7. Joash (40). Faithful to Jehovah while Jehoiada lived. Reforms on all hands.		Slays Ahaziah of Judah. Israel tributary to Assyria. 7th year. Adopts calf worship.	Elisha.	Samas - Ramman IV of Assyria (825–813). Hazael "cuts short" Israel east of Jordan.
815	856	23d year. Death of Jehoiada. Idolatry of Judah. Hazael before Jerusalem, Joash plunders temple to buy him off. 37th year.	Joel.	Hazael's inroads. 11. Jehoahaz (17). Israel delivered into hands of Hazael.		Ramman-nirari III of Assyria (812–784)
798	841	Slain in Millo.	Zechariah.	12. Jehoash (16). Associate with his father first two years.	Elisha.	
797	839	8. Amaziah (29). Defeats Edom. Adopts its idolatry. Defies Israel.	Zechariah stoned.	Three victories over Ben-hadad		Ben-hadad III of Syria.
784	826	Defeated by Jehoash of Israel. Jerusalem plundered and walls broken down. 15th year.		15th year, defeats Judah. Takes Jerusalem.		
783	825	Decline. Amaziah slain by servants in Lachish.		13. Jeroboam II (41). Restored all former boundaries of Israel. Mightiest king of Israel. 27th year.	Jonah.	Shalmaneser III of Assyria (783–774).
780	810	9. Uzziah (52) or Azariah (Chron). Restored Judah's bounds on all sides. Fortified his possessions. 38th year. Judah's prosperity great. 39th year. Uzziah's sacrilege and leprosy. Jotham his son regent.	Zechariah, 2 Chron. xxvi. 5.	(Supposed interregnum of eleven years).	Amos. Hosea.	
743	773			14. Zachariah (6 mo.). Slain by usurper.		Tiglath-pileser II (or Pul) of Assyria (745 –728).
742	772			15. Shallum (1 mo.). Slain by 16. Menahem (10). Tributary to Pul of Assyria.		

Date	Date	Judah	Prophets	Israel		Assyria/Foreign
738						Rezin of Syria.
736	761	50th year.				
	759 758	52d year. 10. Jotham (16). Prosperous reign, 2 Chron. xxvii. 4-6.	Isaiah (758-698). Micah.	17. Pekahiah (2). Slain by his captain, 18. Pekah (20).		
734	742	11. Ahaz (16). Adopted idolatry. Ahaz delivered to Syria and Israel. Captives taken to Samaria and returned. Bounds of Judah cut off on all sides. Submits to Assyria. Foreign altars and idols everywhere. A detestable king.	Oded.	With Rezin of Syria he attacks Judah. 17th year.	Oded.	Damascus taken by Tiglath-pileser.
	740			Israel's northern territory taken by Tiglath-pileser. Servant of Tiglath-pileser. Two and half tribes captured by Assyria. Hoshea, inspired by Assyria, slays Pekah. (Interregnum of eight years.)		
	739			19. Hoshea (9).		
730	730			Confirmed as king by Assyria.		
	728	12. Hezekiah (29). Great religious reforms. Passover observed. Temple service renewed.		3d year. Attempted alliance with So of Egypt. Hoshea imprisoned.		
	724	Land purged of idols.	Isaiah. Micah.	7th year. Samaria besieged by Shalmaneser IV of Assyria.		Shalmaneser IV of Assyria (727-723).
722	722	Revolts against Assyria. 6th year.		9th year. Samaria captured by Sargon. Population deported to foreign districts.		Sargon of Assyria (722-705). Merodach Baladan in Babylon.

SECTION II. — JUDAH ALONE.

Date.	JUDAH.	Prophets.	ASSYRIA AND BABYLON.	Other Peoples.
720		Isaiah.	Sargon captures Karkar.	
717			Sargon destroys the Hittite capital Karkemish.	
714–13	Hezekiah's sickness, Psalm of thanksgiving, Isa. xxxviii. Embassy of Merodach Baladan to Judah.			Medes subject to Sargon.
712			Sargon's capture of Ashdod, Isa. xx. Sargon's overthrow of Babylon.	
711				
710			Death of Sargon; Sennacherib reigns (705-682). War with Merodach Baladan of Babylon.	
705	Judah invaded by Sennacherib. Partial submission of Hezekiah. Disaster to Assyrian army.	Isaiah.		Tirhaka of Egypt.
701				
699	Death of Hezekiah.			
698	13. Manasseh (55). Idolatry rife. Prophets destroyed. Augury practiced. Temple desecrated. Continuation of the rule of Ahaz.		Sennacherib slain by his sons. 2 Kings xix. 37. Esar-haddon of Assyria (681-669).	
681	Dark aves of Judah's history. Manasseh mentioned in a list of tribute-kings as tributary to Esar-haddon.		Esar-haddon conquers Egypt.	
672	Manasseh probably carried to Babylon. Sent back he institutes reforms.			Tirhaka of Egypt. Baal of Tyre.
668			Assurbanipal of Assyria (668-626).	

Date	JUDAH	Prophets		Other Peoples
	Manasseh given in a list of kings tributary to Assurbanipal.			
645	Samaria colonized by importation, Ezra iv. 9.		Assurbanipal plunders Babylon.	664-610 Psammetichus rules in Egypt. Memphis and No-Amon destroyed. Nah. iii. 8-10.
643	14. Amon (2). Idolatrous. Slain in a conspiracy.		Assurbanipal plunders Susa.	
641	15. Josiah (31). Radical reformation begins.			
629	Josiah supported by prophets. Book of the law discovered in the temple.	Jeremiah begins.	Assyrians defeat the Medes.	633 Cyaxares founds Median empire.
624	Passover observed. Temple service re-instituted.	Nahum. Zephaniah. Habakkuk.	Nabo-polassar (625-605) rules Babylonian empire.	Scythian invasion.
610	Josiah slain by Necho of Egypt. 16. Jehoahaz (3 mo.). Deposed by Necho.			
609	17. Jehoiakim (11). Enthroned by Necho. Pays tribute to Egypt.			Necho invades Syria and West Mesopotamia.

SECTION III.—THE EXILE.

Date	JUDAH	Prophets	BABYLON	Other Peoples
606	Jerusalem plundered by Nebukadrezzar, FIRST captivity.		Nineveh falls before Babylonian and Median armies.	Necho defeated at Karkemish.
605			Nebukadrezzar (604-562).	
599	Jerusalem taken and Jehoiakim slain, SECOND captivity.	Ezekiel carried to Babylon. Prophecies (594-572).		

167

Date.	JUDAH.	Prophets.	BABYLON.	Other Peoples.
598	18. Jehoiachin (3 mo.). Rebels and is carried to Babylon by Nebukadrezzar. THIRD captivity.		Nebukadrezzar conquers western rebels.	
597	19. Zedekiah (11). Enthroned by Babylon. Plays fast and loose with Babylon and Egypt.			
589	Jerusalem besieged by Nebukadrezzar.			
587	Jerusalem captured and laid waste by Babylonians. Inhabitants carried to Babylon. FOURTH captivity. Gedaliah governor of remnant. Slain by Ishmael. Johanan carries Jeremiah and others to Egypt.	Jeremiah allowed to remain in Palestine.	Judah captive in Babylon.	
582	Another captivity (FIFTH) of the Jews. Jer. lii. 30.	Jeremiah in Egypt.		
562 561	Jehoiachin (in exile since 598) set free, and honored (2 Kgs. xxv. 27-30.)		Death of Nebukadrezzar; accession of Evil Merodach.	
559			Neriglissar (559-555).	
558 555			Nabonidus (553-538) Belshazzar prince regent.	
537	Jews emancipated.		Cyrus captures Babylon. Darius ruler. Daniel a high official.	Cyrus conquers Media.

1

SECTION IV. — THE RESTORATION.

Date.	JEWS.	Prophets.	PERSIA.	Other Peoples.
536	Jews return under Zerubbabel, according to edict of Cyrus.			
535	Corner-stone of the temple laid. Samaritans' opposition delay the work.		Cambyses (529-522).	
521	Prophets stir up the people to build the temple.	Haggai and Zechariah.	Darius Hystaspes (522-487).	
520	Work resumed.			
517	Temple dedicated.			
478	Events of Esther.		Xerxes (Ahasuerus) (486-466).	Battle of Marathon (490). Battle of Salamis (480).
465			Artaxerxes (465-424) Longimanus.	
458	Second return under Ezra.			
457	Reforms, social and religious.			
446	Nehemiah takes charge of Jews in Palestine. Builds walls of Jerusalem. Law is read.			Herodotus.
434	Sanballat's opposition. Second coming of Nehemiah. Reforms of Ezra and Nehemiah.	Malachi.		Peloponnesian war.
425			Darius II or Ochus. (424-405).	

CLOSE OF THE OLD TESTAMENT.

SECTION V. — THE KINGS OF JUDAH.

Old Date.	KINGS.	Prophets.	Contemporaneous Kings of Israel.
975	1. Rehoboam (17).	Shemaiah, Iddo.	Jeroboam.
957	2. Abijam (3).		"
955	3. Asa (41).	Azariah, Hanani, Jehu.	" Nadab, Baasha, Elah, Zimri, Omri, Ahab.
914	4. Jehoshaphat (25).	Jehu, Jahaziel, Eliezer.	Ahab, Ahaziah, Jehoram.
889	5. Jehoram (8).		Jehoram.
885	6. Ahaziah (1).		"
884	(0) Athaliah (6).	Obadiah.	Jehu.
878	7. Joash (40).	Joel, Zechariah.	" Jehoahaz, Joash.
839	8. Amaziah (29).		Joash, Jeroboam II.
810	9. Uzziah (52).	Zechariah, Joel.	Jeroboam II, Zachariah, Shallum, Menahem, Pekahiah, Pekah.
758	10. Jotham (16).	Isaiah, Micah.	Pekah.
742	11. Ahaz (16).	Oded.	" Hoshea.
728	12. Hezekiah (29).		Hoshea.
698	13. Manasseh (55).		
743	14. Amon (2).	Nahum.	
641	15. Josiah (31).	Jeremiah. Zephaniah.	
610	16. Jehoahaz (3 mo.).		
	17. Jehoiakim (11).	Habakkuk.	
598	18. Jehoiachin (3 mo.).		
	19. Zedekiah (11).		
587	FALL OF JERUSALEM.		

SECTION VI. — THE DYNASTIES OF ISRAEL.

Dynasties.	KINGS.	Prophets.	Contemporaneous Kings of Judah.
First.	1. Jeroboam (22).* 2. Nadab (2).	Ahijah. Iddo.	Rehoboam, Abijah, Asa. "
Second.	3. Baasha (24). 4. Elah (2).	Jehu.	" "
Third.	5. Zimri (7 days).		"
Fourth.	6. Omri (12). 7. Ahab (22). 8. Ahaziah (2). 9. Jehoram (12).	Elijah, Micaiah. Elisha.	" Jehoshaphat. " " Jehoram, Ahaziah.
Fifth.	10. Jehu (28). 11. Jehoahaz (17). 12. Joash (16). 13. Jeroboam II (41). 14. Zachariah (6 mo.).	Jonah. Hosea. Amos.	Joash. " " Amaziah. Amaziah. Uzziah.
Sixth.	15. Shallum (1 mo.).		"
Seventh	16. Menahem (10). 17. Pekahiah (2).		" "
Eighth.	18. Pekah (20).	Oded.	" Jotham, Ahaz.
Ninth.	19. Hoshea (9).		Ahaz, Hezekiah.

* Years of reign.

LIST OF WORKS

QUOTED OR REFERRED TO IN THIS SYLLABUS.

— ALSO A —

SUPPLEMENTAL LIST

Of Works which may be Consulted in a more Comprehensive Study.

B

Baedeker, Syria and the Holy Land. Leipzig, 1885.
Ball, C. J., Prophecies of Jeremiah, Expositor's Bible, New York, 1890.
Barclay, J. T., The City of the Great King. Philadelphia, 1858.
Barrows, E. P., Sacred Geography and Antiquities. American Tract Society, no date.
Bartlett, S. C., Forty Days in the Desert. London, no date.
Besant and Palmer, Jerusalem, the City of Herod and Saladin. New edition, London, 1889.
Bible Atlas and Gazetteer. American Tract Society.
Bible Atlas. New edition, Religious Tract Society, London, 1890.
Bibliotheca Sacra. Andover and Oberlin, 1844-90.
Birks, T. R., The Exodus of Israel. London, 1863.
Bissell, E. C., Biblical Antiquities. American S. S. Union, 1888.
Blaikie, W. G., 1 and 2 Samuel, Expositor's Bible. New York, 1888.
——————— Manual of Bible History. New York, 1882.
Boardman, Geo. D., The Ten Commandments. Philadelphia, 1889.
Briggs, C. A., Messianic Prophecy. New York, 1886.
Brown, Francis, in Old and New Testament Student, Sept. 1884.
Brugsch, H., The Route of the Exodus. Boston, 1880.
By-Paths of Bible Knowledge. Religious Tract Society, London. See Hart, Groser, and Sayce.

C

Cheyne, T. K., Jeremiah, Men of the Bible. New York, 1889.
Coleman, Lyman, An Historical Atlas and Text-Book of Biblical Geography. Philadelphia, 1877.

Conder, C. R., Map of Palestine in 26 Sheets. London, 1880.
———————— Palestine. New York, 1890.

D

Dana, J. D., Bibliotheca Sacra, vols. xiii. xiv and xlii.
———————— Old and New Testament Student, July and Aug. 1890.
Deane, H., Daniel, Men of the Bible. New York, 1889.
Deane, W. J., Abraham, Men of the Bible. New York, 1886.
———————— Samuel and Saul, Men of the Bible. New York, 1889.
———————— David, Men of the Bible. New York, 1889.
———————— Joshua, Men of the Bible. New York, 1890.
Delitzsch, Fried., Wo lag das Paradies? Leipzig, 1881.
Delitzsch, Frz., Old Testament History of Redemption. Leipzig, 1881.
Denio, F. B., in Old and New Testament Student, May 1890.
Dixon, H. W., The Holy Land. London, 1868.
Dods, M., Genesis, Expositor's Bible. New York, 1888.
———————— Isaac, Jacob and Joseph. London, 1887.
Driver, S. R., Isaiah, Men of the Bible. New York, 1888.

E

Ebers, Geo., Durch Gosen zum Sinai. Leipzig, 1872.
Edersheim, A., Bible History, 7 vols. London, no date.
———————— Prophecy and History in Relation to the Messiah. New York, 1885.
Engel, M., Loesung der Paradieses Frage. Leipzig, 1885.
Expositor's Bible Series; see Ball, Blaikie, Dods, Smith, G. A., Watson.

F

Farrar, F. W., Minor Prophets, Men of the Bible. New York, 1890.
———————— Solomon, Men of the Bible. New York, 1889.
Ferguson, J., Ancient Topography of Jerusalem. London, 1847.

G

Gage, W. L., Studies in Bible Lands. American Tract Society.
Geikie, C., Hours with the Bible, 6 vols. New York, 1881–86.
———————— Old Testament Characters. New York, 1885.
Gibson, J. M., The Ages before Moses. New York, 1879.
Green, W. H., The Hebrew Feasts. New York, 1885.

Groser, W. H., Trees and Plants of the Bible. Religious Tract Society, London.
Grove, Geo., Bible Atlas. London, 1868.
Guyot, A., Creation. New York, 1884.

H

Harper, II. A., Bible and Modern Discoveries. Boston, 1889.
Harris, Natural History of the Bible. Boston, 1820.
Hart, H. C., Animals of the Bible. Religious Tract Soc., London.
Hengstenberg, E. W., Egypt and the Books of Moses. Andover, 1843.
——————— on *Balaam* in Commentary on Daniel. Edinburgh, '48.
——————— Genuineness of the Pentateuch, vol. ii.
Howat, H. T., Elijah the Desert Prophet. Edinburgh, 1868.
Humphrey, E. P., Sacred History to Giving the Law. New York, 1888.
Hurlbut, J. L., Manual of Biblical Geography. Chicago, 1887.
——————— Solomon's Temple, Old Testament Student, Dec. '87.

J

Johnson, T. R., Biblical Wall Atlas. Chicago and New York, 1889.
Josephus, Antiquities of the Jews.

K

Kellogg, A. H., Abraham, Moses and Joseph in Egypt. New York, 1887.
Kennedy, J. F., Countries and Places Mentioned in Bible History American S. S. Union, no date.
Kiepert, H., Neue Wandkarte von Palaestina. Berlin, 1854.
Krummacher, F. W., David, King of Israel. Edinburgh, 1867.
Kurtz, J. H., History of the Old Covenant. Edinburgh, 1859.

L

Lenormant, F., Beginnings of History. New York, 1886.
Lynch, W.F., Expedition to the Jordan and Dead Sea. Philadelphia, 1849.

M

Macduff, J. R., Sunsets on Hebrew Mountains. New York, 1862.
MacGregor, J., The Rob Roy on the Jordan, Nile and Red Sea. New York, 1870.
Manning, S., Those Holy Fields. London, Relig. Tract Soc., no date.
Men of the Bible Series; see Cheyne, Deane, H., Deane, W. J., Driver, Farrar, Milligan, Rawlinson.

Merrill, S., East of the Jordan. New York, 1883.
Meyer, F. B., Israel, a Prince with God. Chicago, 1890.
——————— Abraham; or the Obedience of Faith. Chicago, '90.
Miller, Hugh, Testimony of the Rocks. Boston, 1857.
Milligan, W., Elijah, Men of the Bible. New York, 1889.
Mozley, J. B., Lectures on the Old Testament. London, 1884.

N

North American Review, 1882.
Northrup, G. W., on Extermination of the Canaanites, in "The Standard," April 21, 1881.

O

Oehler, G., Old Testament Theology, Day's Translation. New York.
Old Testament Student. 1881–90.
Orelli, C. von, Old Testament Prophecy. Edinburgh, 1885.
Osborn, H. S., Wall Map of Palestine. Oxford, O.
——————— Guide to Palestine. Philadelphia, 1868.
——————— Plants of the Bible. Philadelphia, 1865.

P

Palmer, E. H., The Desert of the Exodus, 2 vols. Cambridge, '71.
Perrot and Chipiez, Le Temple Jerusalem restitutes. Paris, 1889.
Porter, J. L., Giant Cities of Bashan. New York, 1866.
Price, Ira M., "Schools of the Sons of the Prophets," in Old Test. Student, March 1889.
——————— "Lost Writings in Old Testament," in Bibliotheca Sacra, April, 1889.
——————— Syllabus of the Minor Prophets. Saylor Springs, Ill., 1890.

R

Rawlinson, G., The Five Great Monarchies of the Ancient Eastern World, 3 vols. London, 1879.
——————— Moses, Men of the Bible. New York, 1888.
——————— Kings of Israel and Judah, Men of the Bible. New York, 1889.
Records of the Past, 2d series. London, 1888—.
Renouf, L. P., The Religion of Ancient Egypt. New York, no date. (Hibbert Lectures, 1879).
Ritter, C., Geography of Palestine, 4 vols. New York, 1868.
Robinson, Edw., Biblical Researches in Palestine. Boston, 1857.
——————— Physical Geography of Palestine. Boston, 1865.

Sayce, A. H., Fresh Light from Ancient Monuments. London, 1885.
——————— The Hittites. Religious Tract Society, London, 1888.
——————— The Times of Isaiah. London, 1889.
Schodde, G. H., The Book of Enoch. Andover, 1882.
Schrader, E., Cuneiform Inscriptions and the Old Testament. Trans. by O. C. Whitehouse, 2 vols. London, 1885-88.
Schumacher, G., Across the Jordan. London, 1887.
Smith, G. A., Isaiah, Expositor's Bible, vol. i. New York, 1889.
Smith's Dictionary of the Bible, 4 vols. Boston, 1878.
Smith, W., Old Testament History. New York, 1881.
Stanley, A. P., History of the Jewish Church, 3 vols. New York, 1884.
——————— Sinai and Palestine. New York, 1885.

T

Taylor, W. M., David, King of Israel. New York, 1883.
Thomson, Wm., The Land and The Book, 3 vols. New edition, New York, 1886.
Thrupp, Ancient Jerusalem, a new Investigation, 1885.
Tomkins, H. G., The Times of Abraham. London, 1878.
Transactions of the Society of Biblical Archæology. London,'71—.
Tristram, H. B., The Land of Moab. New York, 1873.
——————— The Land of Israel. New York, 1886.
——————— Natural History of the Bible. New York, 1867.
——————— Fauna and Flora of Palestine. London, 1888.

V

Van de Velde, C. W. M., Map of the Holy Land in eight sheets. 2d edition, London, 1865.

W

Wallace, A., The Desert and The Holy Land. Edinburgh, 1868.
Warren, W. F., Paradise Found: the Cradle of the Human Race at the North Pole. Boston, 1885.
Watson, R. A., Judges and Ruth, Expositor's Bible. New York, 1890.
Wilberforce, S., Heroes of Hebrew History. New York, 1870.
Williams, Geo., The Holy City, 2 vols. London, 1849.
Wilson, John, The Lands of the Bible, 2 vols. Edinburgh, 1847.
Wilson and Warren, The Recovery of Jerusalem. New York, 1871.
Wood, J. G., Bible Animals. New York, 1872.
Wright, Zechariah and his Prophecies. New York.

SUPPLEMENTAL LIST,

FOR FURTHER STUDY.

A dash after a date indicates that the work is still publishing.

Alker, E., Chronologie der Buecher der Koenige und Paralipomenon. Leipzig, 1889.
Andrews, E. B., History, Prophecy and Gospel. Boston, 1890.
Baethgen, F., Beitraege zur semitischen Religions-geschichte. Berlin, 1888.
Bartlett and Peters, The Scriptures, Hebrew and Christian. 2 vols. Philadelphia, 1887–90.
Beecher, W. J., The Historical Situation in Joel and Obadiah, Journal of Soc. Bib. Lit. and Exegesis, June and Dec. 1888.
Boscawen, W. St. C., The Kerubim in Eden, in Bab. and Orient. Record, June 1886.
Brugsch, H., History of Egypt under the Pharaohs. Trans. from the German by Philip Smith. 2d edition, 2 vols., London, 1881.
Budde, K., Die Biblische Urgeschichte [Gen. i—xii. 5] untersucht Giessen, 1883.
Budge, E. A. W., The Dwellers on the Nile. London, Religious Tract Society, 1885.
Cambridge Bible for Schools and Colleges. Cambridge, 1883—.
Cave, A. B., The Scriptural Doctrine of Sacrifice and Atonement. New edition, New York, 1890.
Cheyne, T. K., The Hallowing of Criticism; nine sermons on Elijah, etc. London, 1888.
Conder, C. R., Tent Work in Palestine. New edition, London, '89.
Crane, O. T., The Samaritan Chronicle; or the Book of Joshua, son of Nun. New York, 1890.
Davis, J. D., The Babylonian Flood-Legend and the Hebrew Record of the Deluge, in Presbyterian Review, July 1889.
Dawson, J. W., Modern Science in Bible Lands. New York, 1889.
——————— Origin of the World. New York, no date.
——————— Nature and the Bible. New York, 1875.
Duncker, M., Geschichte des Alterthums. Baende ii. u. iii., 5te Aufl. Leipzig, 1878-82.

Ebers, Geo., Joshua, a Biblical Picture. New York, 1890.
Edersheim, E. W., Laws and Polity of the Jews. London, 1883.
Edwards, A. B., Bubastis, in The Century, Jan. 1890.
Egypt Exploration Fund, Quarterly Statements of the. London.
Ewald, H., The History of Israel, 7 vols. Trans. from the German. London, 1871.
Gibson, J. M., The Mosaic Era. New York, 1881.
Godet, F., Studies in the Old Testament. 2d edition, London, 1883.
Graetz, H., Geschichte der Juden von der aeltesten Zeiten bis auf die Gegenwart, 11 Baende, 2 aufl. Leipzig, 1864-1870.
Green, W. H., Moses and the Prophets. New York, 1883.
Griffis, W. E., The Lily among Thorns. Boston, 1889.

Hengstenberg, E. W., History of the Kingdom of God under the Old Testament. Trans. from the German, 2 vols. Edinburgh, 1871-73.
Hommel, F., Geschichte Babyloniens und Assyriens. Berlin, 1885-88.

Jost, J. M., Geschichte des Judenthums und seiner Secten. 3 Baende. Leipzig, 1857-59.

Kamphausen, A., Die Chronologie d. Heb. Koenige. Bonn, 1883.
Kellner, M. L., The Deluge in the Izdubar Epic and in the Old Testament, in The Church Review, 1888.
Kittel, R., Geschichte der Hebræer. Gotha, 1888—
Koehler, S., Lehrbuch der biblischen Geschichte Alten Testaments. Erlangen, 1889—
Koenig, F. E., The Religious History of Israel. New York, 1886.
Kuenen, A., The Religion of Israel to the Fall of the Jewish State. 3 vols. London, 1874-75.

Lacouperie, T. de, The Tree of Life and the Calendar Plant of Babylonia and China, in Bab. and Orient. Record, June 1888.
Lansing, J. G., The Egyptian Nile as a Civilizer. Presby. Rev , Apr. 1889.
Layard, A. H., Nineveh and its Remains, 2 vols. New York, 1849.
Layard, A. H., Nineveh and Babylon. London, 1853.
Loftus, W. K., Travels and Researches in Chaldæa and Susiana. New York, 1857.

SUPPLEMENTAL LIST. 179

Macduff, J. R., The Prophet of Fire (Elijah). New York, 1868.
Martin, H., The Prophet Jonah: his Character and Mission to Nineveh. Edinburgh, 1889.
McCausland, D., Adam and the Adamite. London, 1872.
Miller, W., The Least of all Lands; chapter on the Topography of Palestine in relation to its History. London, 1888.
Milman, H. H., The History of the Jews. 3 vols. New York, 1882.
Meyer, Ed., Geschichte des Alterthums. 1 Band; bis zur Begruendung des Perserreichs. Stuttgart, 1884.
Moore, W. W., The Discovery of Pithom, in Presby. Quar., April 1889.

Osborn, H. S., Biblical History and Geography. American Tract Society, 1890.

Paine, J. A., The Pharaoh of the Exodus and his Son, in The Century, Sept. 1889.
Palestine Exploration Fund, Quarterly Statements of. London, 1873—
Peitschmann, Geschichte der Phœnizier. Berlin, 1888—
Proceedings of the Society of Biblical Archæology. London, 1881-90.

Ragozin, Z. A., Assyria, Story of the Nations. New York, 1887.
———— Chaldea, Story of the Nations. New York, 1886.
———— Media, Babylonia and Persia. New York, 1888.
Rawlinson, Geo., Biblical Topography. New York, 1887.
———— Ancient Egypt, Story of the Nations. New York, 1887.
———— History of Phœnicia. London, 1889.
———— Phœnicia, Story of the Nations. New York, 1888.
———— Isaac and Jacob, Men of the Bible. New York, 1890.
Renan, E., History of the People of Israel, 2 vols. issued. Boston, 1888—
Riehm, E., Handwoerterbuch des biblischen Alterthums. Leipzig, 1878-84.
Robinson, C. S., The Pharaohs of the Bondage and the Exodus. New York, 1887.

Sayce, A. H., The Ancient Empires of the East. New York, 1886.

———— The White Race of Ancient Palestine, Expositor, July 1888.
Schaff, P., Through Bible Lands. New York, 1889.
Smith Geo., Assyrian Discoveries: an Account of Explorations and Discoveries on the site of Nineveh during 1873 and 1874. Edited by A. H. Sayce. New York, 1875.
———— The Chaldaean Account of Genesis. Edited by A. H. Sayce. New York, 1880.
Smith, H. P., The High Places. Heb. Student, April 1883.
Smith, W. R., Old Testament in the Jewish Church. New York, 1881.
———— The Prophets of Israel. New York, 1882.
Stade, B., Geschichte des Volkes Israel. Berlin, 1881—

Taylor, W. M., Elijah the Prophet. New York, 1885.
———— Moses the Lawgiver. New York, 1878.
———— Daniel the Beloved. New York, 1879.
Tiele, C. P.. Babylonisch-Assyrische Geschichte. Gotha, 1886-88.
Trumbull, H. C., Kadesh Barnea. New York, 1884.
———— The Blood Covenant. New York, 1885.

Victoria Institute, Transactions of the. London.
Vigoureaux, F., La Bible et les Decouvertes modernes en Palestine, en Egypte et en Assyrie. 5 ed. 4 Tom. Paris, 1888.
———— Melanges Bibliques, La Cosmogonie mosaiques d'apres les Peres de l'Eglise, suivie d'etudes diverses relatives a l'Ancien et au Nouveau Testament. 2e ed. Paris, 1889.

Ward, E. S. P. and H. D., The Master of the Magicians. Boston, 1890.
Wellhausen, J., The History of Israel. Edinburgh, 1885.
Wiedemann, A., Aegyptische Geschichte. Gotha, 1886—
Wilkinson, J. G., Manners and Customs of the Ancient Egyptians. New edition by Samuel Birch, 3 vols. London, 1878.
Wilson, Edw. L., In Scripture Lands. New York, 1890.
Zeitschrift fuer d. Alttest. Wissenschaft. Herausg. von B. Stade, 1880—

1

GENERAL INDEX.

PROPER NAMES AND TOPICS.

Numbers refer to pages.

AARON AND MOSES, 49-59
Abdon, twelfth judge, 76
Abel, first martyr, 31; city of, 95
Abiathar, priest, 96
Abigail, wife of Nabal, 89
Abijah, son of Jeroboam I, 104
Abijam, king of Judah, 104-5
Abimelech and Abraham, 42
Abimelech, son of Gideon, 74-5
Abiram and Dathan, 58
Abishai, brother of Joab, 94
Abner, captain, 91
Abraham's career, 40-43
Absalom, son of David, 94
Achan, 64
Achish, king in Philistia, 89
Adam and Eve, 29-30
Adoni-bezek, 70
Adonijah son of David, 95
Adullam, cave of, 87
Agag, king of Amalek, 85
Age of the world. 27
Ahab, king of Israel, 109-10; 145
Ahava, river, 158
Ahaz, king of Judah, 102, 127-8, 135; altars of, removed, 138
Ahaziah, king of Judah, 119
Ahaziah, son of Ahab, king of Israel, 110, 116
Ahijah, the Shilonite, 92, 103
Ahithophel, counsellor, 94
Ai, city of, 64
Altar, first, 35
Amalek(ites), 53, 72, 82, 85, 90
Amasa, captain, 94-95
Amaziah, king of Judah, 20, 123

Ammon, 72, 85, 97; subdued, 127; 147
Ammonite oppression, 75-6; war, 81, 84, 92
Amnon, son of David, 94
Amon, king of Judah, 136
Amorites, 61
Amos, prophet, 128
Anakim, 66
Angel of Jehovah, 42
Ante-diluvian period, 24, 27-33
Antiochus Epiphanes, 20
Aphek, Ahab's victory at, 110
Arabah, sea of the, 14, 123
Arabian desert, 37
Arabians plunder Jerusalem, 20, 113
Aram, 37
Ark, Noah's, 34
Armenia, 29, 36, 37
Arnon, from Sinai to the, 57-61
Arpachshad, 37
Artaxerxes, 158
Asa, king of Judah, 106-7
Asaph, singer, 92, 130
Ashdod, 79; captured, 132
Asher, tribe of, 68, 131
Asherah, 400 prophets of, 118; cut down, 130; 136, 138
Asherim, idols, 106, 112
Ashkelon, city of, 77
Asia Minor, 36
Assyria, relations to, 37, 110
Athaliah, usurper, 120-1, 136
Atmosphere of Palestine, 16
Augury and enchantments, 136
Azariah(-Uzziah), king of Judah, 124
Azariah, son of Oded, 106, 114

BAAL WORSHIP established, 109-10, 136; idols destroyed, 138
Baal worshippers slaughtered, 120
Baal-gad, 71
Baal Peor, 60
Baal-zebub, 110
Baal Zephon, 52
Baasha, king of Israel, 106-7
Babel, tower of, 38
Babylon captured, 153
Babylonian exile, 149-51
Balaam, 59
Bamoth Baal, 59
Barak, 73
Baruch, Jeremiah's scribe, 148
Barzillai, 70, 94, 96
Bashan, 13, 39
Bath-sheba, 93
Beer-sheba, 18, 131; origin of, 42; 81; Elijah at, 115
Beginning, second, 35
Belial, 78
Belshazzar, feast of, 152
Ben-hadad of Syria, 106, 110
Benjamin, territory of, 68
Berothai, 92
Betah, 92
Bethel, 18; Abraham at, 40; Jacob at, 45; 70, 71, 81, 99; Elijah at, 110; school at, 117
Beth-horon, 65
Bethlehem, 83, 147
Beth-shemesh, 79
Bible, books of the, 21
Birs-Nimroud, 38
Boaz, 70, 78, 101
Bondage, period of, 24, 48-50
Books of the Bible, 21
" " Old Testament, 21
" and chapters in O. T., 21-2
Botany of Palestine, 15
Brooks of Palestine, 14

CAIN, 31-2
Caleb, 67
Calf, golden, 55
Cambyses, 155
Campaign, southern, 64; northern, 66
Canaan, 12; entrance into, 63
Canaan's (son of Ham) curse, 36
Canaanites, extermination of, 66-7, 70
Captivity, period of the, 25
Caravan, of returning exiles, 154
Carmel, 18, 71; Elijah at, 109; Elisha at, 116; school at, 117
Carthaginians, 73
Chaldeans, slain at Mizpah, 147
Chebar, river, 180
Cherith, Elijah at, 115
Cherubim in Old Testament, 31
Chinnereth, sea of, 14
Circumcision, rite of, 42
City, first, 32
Classical history, beginning of, 153
Climate of Palestine, 16
Commandments, ten, 55; commentary on, 61
Confusion of tongues, 38
Conquest, period of the, 24, 63-71
Conquests, east of the Jordan, 59-61
Covenant, God's, with Noah, 35
Creation, 27-9; legends of, 27
Cressy, 73
Cush, 37

DAGON, god of Philistia, 79
Damascus, 29
Dan, 18; territory of, 68; 70, 131
Daniel, in Babylon, 150-2
Darius (II) Hystaspes, 156, 158
Dathan and Abiram, 58
David's career, 82-96
Dead Sea, 14
Deborah, Rebekah's nurse, 46
" prophetess, 73; song, 74
Delilah, 77
Deluge, cause, time, duration, universality, object, traditions of, 34-35
Dial of Ahaz, 133
Dinah, 45
Dispersion, tower of Babel and the, 37

PROPER NAMES AND TOPICS. 183

Division of the kingdom, 103
Divisions, political, of Palestine, 17
Doeg, Edomite, 86
Dothan, siege of, 111
Drunkenness, first, 36
Dual kingdom, period of the, 25

EASTERN SEA, 14

Ebal, Mt., 62, 64
Ebenezer, 81
Eden, garden of, 29
Edict of Cyrus, 153; renewed by Darius II, 155
Edom, 58, 85, 92, 97, 147
Edomites, revolt, 119
Eglon, king of Moab, 72
Egypt, Abraham's sojourn in, 40; Jacob's appeal to, 47; settlement in, 48; religion of, 49; Solomon's commerce with, 98; flight of the remnant to, 148; Ezekiel's prophecy concerning fate of, 148
Ehud, second judge, 72, 73
Ekron, Philistine city, 79
Elah, king of Israel, 107
Elam, country, 37
Elamite powers, rise of Persian and, 152
Elath restored, 124
Eleazar, priest, 60
Eli and fall of Shiloh, 78-80
Eliakim (Jehoiakim), 140
Eliezer, prophet, 112
Elijah, prophet, 109-10, 115-16
Elim, in wilderness, 52-3
Elon, eleventh judge, 76
Emancipation of Jewish slaves, 153
Embassies to Babylon, 143
Endor, witch of, 83, 87
Engedi, 87; Jehoshaphat's victory at, 113
Enoch, book of, 33
Entanglements with Egypt, Zedekiah's, 143
Ephraim, territory of, 68, 131
Esar-haddon, king of Assyria, 136
Esau and Jacob, 44
Esdraelon, plain of 12
Esther, 78; story and book, 156-7

Etam, 77
Etham, 51
Ethiopians, war with Asa, 106, 132
Euphrates, river, 37
Eve, Adam and, 29, 30
Exile, period of, 25, 145-151; Babylonian, 149-51
Exiles, classes of, condition of, 150; number, return, 154
Exodus, 50-1
Ezekiel, prophet, 150-2
Ezion Geber, 59
Ezra, scribe, 150-60

FALL, TEMPTATION and, 30-31

Fall of Babylon, 141
" Jerusalem, 141
" Samaria, 129-32
Feasts, 55
Flaming Sword, 31
Foods prohibited and permitted, 56

GAD, ALLOTMENT to, 60

Gad the seer, 87
Galilee, 12
Galilee, sea of, 14
Gath, 79, 87, 122
Gaza, 65, 77
Geba, 84
Gedaliah, governor in Palestine, 147
Gehazi, 116
Genesis I-II. 3, object of, 28; beginnings in, 28; and geology, 27
Geology of Palestine, 15
Gerar, Isaac in, 54
Gerizim, 62, 138
Geshur, 44
Gibbethon, Philistine fortress, 107
Gibeon's deceit, 64, 65
Gibeonites, 66, 95
Gideon, fifth judge, 74
Gilboa, Mt., 18, 87
Gilead, 15, 45
Gilgal, 63, 81, 83; Elijah at, 116; school at, 117
Goliath, 86, 89
Goshen, land of, 48

Gozan, 130
Greece, in Europe, 36
Gur-baal, Arabian city, 124

HABAKKUK, PROPHET, 141
Habor, 130
Hachilah, 87
Hadadezer of Zobah, 92
Hagar, story of, 42
Haggai, prophet, 155
Halah, 130
Ham and descendants, 37
Haman, the Agagite, 157
Hamath, 37
Hanani the seer, 106, 114
Hannah, 78, 80
Haran, 37, 40, 41, 45
Hauran, 15
Hazael of Syria, 120, 121
Hazeroth, 57
Hazor, 18, 66
Hebrew poetry, 32
Hebron, 18, 65, 66, 68, 90
Hejaz, 37
Heman, 83, 92
Hereth, forest of, 87
Heshbon, 18, 59
Hezekiah, king of Judah, 102, 129-134, 145
High places, 112, 136; in Samaria, Simeon, Naphtali, 138
Hinnom, valley of, 136
Hiram of Tyre, 91
Hittites, 37, 44, 97
Holy of holies, 55
Holy Land, 12
Hophra, king of Egypt, 143
Hor, Mt., 58
Horeb, Mt., Moses in, 53; Elijah at, 115
Horses, first use of, 66
Hoshea, king of Israel, 126, 129
Host of heaven worshipped, 136
Huldah, prophetess, 139, 145
Hur, Aaron and, 55
Hushai, 94
Hystaspes, Darius (II), 156

IBZAN, TENTH JUDGE, 76
Institutions during the exile, 150-1
Isaac, sacrifice of, career of, 43
Isaiah, prophet, 128; to Hezekiah, 145, 149
Ish-bosheth, 91
Ishmael, birth of, 42
Ishmael, seed-royal, murderer of Gedaliah, 147
Israel, Jacob named, 45
Israel, introduction to, history of, Gen. i—xi. 9
Issachar, territory of, 68, 131
Ittai, 94

JABESH, 87
Jachin, pillar, 101
Jacob's wanderings, 45-46
Jacob and Esau, 44
Jahaziel, prophet, 113
Jair, eighth judge, 76
Japheth's part in Shem's God, 36
Jashar, book of, 65, 90
Jebus, conquest of, 90
Jebusites, 20
Jeduthun, 92
Jehoahaz, king of Israel, 121
" " Judah, 140
Jehoiachin, king of Judah, 20, 142, 149
Jehoiada, high priest, 121
Jehoiakim, king of Judah, 20, 140-1, 145, 149
Jehonadab, son of Rechab, 120
Jehoram, king of Judah, 20, 116, 119
Jehoram, son of Ahab, king of Israel, 110-11
Jehoshaphat, king of Judah, 110, 112-13 145
Jehu, son of Hanani, prophet, 112
Jehu, king of Israel, 117, 120
Jephthah, ninth judge, 76
Jeremiah, prophet, 139
Jericho, 14, 18; destruction of, 64; Elijah at, 116; school at, 117
Jeroboam I, king of Israel, 103-6, 138
" II, " " 123
Jerusalem, 18; names, location, 19; history of, 20; ownership, 68; 78; de-

PROPER NAMES AND TOPICS. 185

struction, 136; captivity, 142; five captivities of, by Nebukadrezzar, 146; walls rebuilt, 159
Jesse, father of David, 82
Jethro, father-in-law to Moses, 49, 54
Jews slain at Mizpah, 147
Jezebel, Ahab's wife, 109-10; slain, 120; cf. 136
Jezreel, Ahaziah of Judah at, 120
Joab, David's general, 91, 96
Joash of Israel, 20, 102, 122
" Judah, 121; law at coronation of, 138
Johanan, of remnant in Palestine, 147
Jonah's message to Jeroboam II, 123
Jonathan, 84-6
Joppa, city, 18
Jordan, river, 13-4
Joseph sold in Egypt, 46; imprisoned and promoted, 47; bones buried, 70
Joshua, 53, 63
Josiah, king of Judah, 102; career of, 137-9
Jotham, king of Judah, 126-7
Jubilee year, 57
Judah, sin of, 45; territory of, 68
Judah alone, period of, 25.
Judea, 12
Judges, period of, 25, 72-83

KADESH BARNEA, 58, 65
Kadesh, wilderness of, 61
Karkar, 110
Kibroth-Hataavah, 57
Keilah, 87
Kingdom, period of the, 25, 84-102
" " " dual, 25, 103—128
Kings of the east, invasion by, 41
Kirjath-jearim, 80, 91
Korah, and his host, 58; 92

LABAN AND JACOB, 45
Lachish, 65
Laish, 79
Lakes of Palestine, 14
Lamech's song and the origin of the arts, 32

Languages, origin of different, 38
Law found in the temple, 138
Leah and Rachel, 45
Lebanon, 12, 37
Levites, work of, 57
Liberty, beginning of religious, 153
Libnah, 65; revolt of, 119
Longevity of the ante-diluvians, 33
Lot and Abraham, 40, 41
" and destruction of Sodom, 42
Lud, Lydians, 37

MACPELAH, CAVE of, 43
Mahanaim, city or camp, 18, 91, 94
Makkedah, Canaanitish city, 65
Mamre, oaks of, 41
Man, creation of, 27-9; antiquity of, 29
Manasseh, tribe, 60; king of Judah, 102; 131; career of, 135-6; altars of, removed 138, 145
Manna, food, 53
Manoah, 76
Maon, 87
Marah, waters of, 53
Marathon, battle of, 156
March to the sea, 51; to Sinai, 53
Marriages, mixed, condemned, 158-9
Mattaniah, see Zedekiah.
Medes, captives of Israel with the, 130
Mediterranean sea, 12, 14, 37
Melchi-shua, son of Saul, 88
Melchizekek, 41
Menahem, king of Israel, 126, 128
Menzaleh, lake, 52
Mephibosheth, of Saul, 94
Merari, 92
Merib-baal, son of Saul, 88
Merodach-Baladan king of Babylon, 133
Merom, lake, 14, 66
Mesha, king of Moab, 109, 113
Mesopotamia, 37; invasion by kings of, 72
Micah, prophet, 70, 128; to Judah, 149
Micaiah, prophet, 110
Michal, 86
Michmash, 84
Midian, 49

Midianite oppression, 74
Migdol, 52
Miriam, Moses' sister, 52, 57
Mizpah, 147
Mizpeh, 71, 76, 80, 81, 83, 87
Mizraim (Egypt), 57
Moab, 72, 85, 147
Moloch, 127
Mordecai, 157
Moriah, Mt., 43, 100
Moses' training, 49; appeal to Pharaoh, 49, 50; leadership of Israel, 50-62
Murder, first, 32

NAAMAH, 97
Naaman the Syrian, 116
Nabal, 89
Naboth, 70, 110
Nadab, king of Israel, 107
Nahor, 44
Nahum, 139
Naioth, 86
Naphtali, territory of, 68
Nathan, the prophet, 92, 93
Natural History of Palestine, 15
Nazarite, 57, 77, 80
Nebukadrezzar, 20, 102; at Jerusalem, 143
Nebuzaradan's destruction of Jerusalem, 146
Necho, expedition through Palestine, 139
Nehemiah, 20; third return under, 158-60
New Testament period, political divisions in, 17
Nimrod, 27
Noah's prophecy, 35
Nob, 86
North pole, Eden at, 29

OBADIAH, AHAB'S servant, 109
Obed-edom, 91
Obelisks broken, 130
Oded, father of Azariah, 106
Oded, a prophet ro Israel, 127
Offerings, significance of the, 56
Og, king of Bashan, 59, 61
Old Testament world, 10
    "   "   books of, 21
    "   "   history, periods of, 24-25

Omri, king of Israel, 109; house of Omri extirpated, 120
Oppression, first Philistine, 73; Moabite, 72; Canaanite, 73; Midianite, 74
Oriental history, end of, 153
Ornan, 95
Orpah, 77
Othniel, first judge, 73
Outfit for Old Testament study, 23

PADDAN-ARAM, 44
Palestine, geography, 11-15; name, 12; plains, 13; lakes, 14; sea, brooks, 14; political divisions, 17; possessors of, at return of exiles, 154
Paran, wilderness, 58
Passover established, 51; observed, 57, 139
Patriarchal period, 40-47; political divisions in, 17
Pekah, king of Israel, 126, 128
Pekahiah, king of Israel, 126
Penuel, Jacob at, 45
Peor, 59
Periods of time in Bible, 24
Periods of Old Testament History, 24-25
Persian and Elamite powers, rise of, 152
Pharaoh and Abraham, 40; and Jacob, 48; and Moses, 42-62
Philistia, 12
Philistines, plunder Jerusalem, 20; 43, 95
Phœnicia, 12
Pi-hahiroth, 52
Pisgah, 59, 62
Plagues in Egypt, 50, 51
Plains of Palestine, 14
Polygamy, first, 32
Post-diluvian period, 24, 34-39
Potiphar, 47
Prediction, first, by man, 36
Prophets, schools of the, 82
Pul, see Tiglath-pileser.
Punishment of serpent, Adam and Eve, 30
Punishment, capital, established, 35
Purification, laws of, 56
Purim, feast of, 157
Purity of atmosphere in Palestine, 16

PROPER NAMES AND TOPICS. 187

Put, or Punt, 37

QUAILS, SURFEIT of, 57
Queen of Sheba, 99

RABBAH, 92
Rachel and Leah, 45
Racial affinity, scientific evidences of, 37
Rahab, 63, 64
Rain in Palestine, 16
Ramah, 81, 83, 106; school at, 117
Rameses to Succoth, 51
Ramoth Gilead, 18, 110, 112
Rebekah, finding of, 43
Rechab, 120
Red Sea to Arnon, 59
Reforms of Ezra and Nehemiah, 159
Refuge, cities of, 60; east of Jordan, 61
Regal period, political divisions in, 17
Rehoboam, 20, 97, 102; career of, 103-4
Remnants in Palestine, and Egypt, 147-9
Rephidim, 53
Restoration, period of, 25, 152-60
Return, first, 153-4; second, under Ezra, 157-8; third, Nehemiah, 158-60
Reuben, Gad and half-tribe of Manasseh, 70
Review, general, 160-1
Rezin of Syria leagued with Pekah against Ahaz, 126
Riblah, Zedekiah condemned at, 146
Roll cut by Jehoiakim, 141
Ruth, 70, 77, 78

SABBATH, ORIGIN and significance of, 28; desecration, 159
Sabbatical year, 57
Sacrifice, 35; human, in Old Testament, 43
Salt Sea, 14
Samaria, 12, 18, 68; Elisha at, 116; besieged by Syrians, 117; fall of, 129 sq.
Samaritans, origin of, 130; delayed temple building, 154-5
Samson, thirteenth judge, 76
Samuel's career, 80-3

Sanballat's opposition to Nehemiah, 159
Sarah, wife of Abraham, 43
Sargon, king of Assyria, 129; invasion of, 132
Saul's career; 81-8
Schools of the sons of the prophets, 117
Sea of Palestine, 14
Seasons of Palestine, 16
Semitic sway, end of, 153
Sennacherib, king of Assyria, 132; invasion of, 134
Serpent, 30; Moses', destroyed, 130
Seth, descendants of, 323
Settlement of the tribes, 67
Seventh day, 27
Shallum, king of Israel, 124-6
Shalmaneser II, 110
" IV, 129
Shamgar, third judge, 73
Shamir, 75
Sharon, 12
Sheba, son of Bichri, 45
Shechem, 18; first altar in Canaan at, 40 Jacob at, 45; 68, 70, 74; Rehoboam at 103, 147
Shemaiah, prophet, 105
Shem's future, 36
" descendants, 37, 40
Shibboleth, 76
Shiloh, 68, 79, 80, 82, 109
Shimei 94, 96
Shinar, 37, 38
Shishak, 20; 102
Shunem, 87; Elisha at, 116
Shur, 53
Shushan, 37
Siege of Jerusalem, 146
Sihon, king of Amorites, 59
Simeon, tribe, 68
Sin, wilderness of, 53
Sin of Adam and Eve, 30
Sinai, march to, 53; doings at in Exodus, 54; to the Arnon, 57
Sisera, 73
Smerdis false, 156
So, king of Egypt, 129

Sodom, fate of, 42
Sodomites removed, 106, 138
Sojourn in Egypt, 49
Solomon's career, 95-9; high places of Solomon, 138; 145
Solomon's temple, 99-102
Song of Moses, 62
Sons of God and daughters of men, 34
South country, 12, 15, 40, 65
Spies' work, 58
Succoth, 51
Sun, images, 138; horses and chariots of the, 138
Sun standing still, 65
Susa, 156, 158
Sword, flaming, 31
Synagogue, origin of, 160
Syria, upper, 37
Syrians, 92

TABERAH, 57

Tabernacle, 55, 100
Table of nations, 36
Tabor, Mt., 71
Tahpahnes, Jeremiah at, 148
Tarshish, ships of, 98, 112
Temperature of Palestine, 16
Temple, Solomon's, 99-102; repaired,138; corner-stone of second, 154; building of second, 155-6
Temptation and fall, 30-1
Thebez, 75
Tibni and Omri, 108.
Tiglath-pileser, 126, 129
Tigris, river, 37
Time, periods of, covered by the Bible, 24
Time, periods of, between Adam and the deluge, 33
Timnath-Serah, 69
Tiphsah smitten, 126
Tirzah, capital of Israel, 107
Tobiah, the Ammonite, 159
Toi of Hamath, 92
Tola, seventh judge, 75
Tophet, 136, 138

Tower of Babel, 38
Tribal period, political divisions in, 17
Tribes, settlement of, in Canaan, 67
Tyre, 18, 154

UR OF THE CHALDEES, 40, 41
Urijah, prophet, 141
Urim, 87
Uzzah, 91
Uzziah, king of Judah, 124, 125, 128

VASHTI, queen of Persia, 157

WADIES OF PALESTINE, 14
Wall, writing on the, 152
Walls of Jerusalem rebuilt, 159
Wanderings, period of, 24, 51-62
War, civil, 77
Wars of Jehovah, book of, 59
Why study O. T. History? 5-9
Wilderness, 53; of Sin, 53; of Paran, 58
Winds of Palestine, 16

XERXES (Ahasuerus), 158

YEARS, sabbatical and jubilee, 57

ZAREPHATH, Elijah at, 115
Zachariah, son of Jeroboam II, king of Israel, 124
Zebulon, territory of, 68; 131
Zechariah, prophet stoned by Joash of Judah, 121
Zechariah, prophet under Uzziah of Judah, 124
Zechariah, prophet, contemporary of Haggai, 155
Zedekiah, 20, 142-3, 145
Zephaniah, 139
Zerubbabel, leader of returning exiles, 154
Ziba, 94
Ziklag, 89
Zimri, 7-day-king of Israel, 107
Zin, wilderness of, 58
Ziph, wilderness of, 87
Zobah, 85
Zoology of Palestine, 15

INDEX OF SCRIPTURE TEXTS.

	PAGES.		PAGES.
GENESIS i—ii. 3	27	xlvi—l.	48
ii. 4-25	29	xlix. 17	30
iii.	30		
iv. 3, 4	90	**EXODUS** i. 8—vii. 13	49
v.	33	vii. 14—x. 29	50
vi.—viii. 14	34	ix. 9 sq.	133
viii. 15—ix. 29	35	xi.—xiv. 14	51
viii. 20	99	xiv. 15—xv. 21	52
ix. 5	31	xv. 22—xviii. 27	53
x.	36, 37	xviii—xix	54
xi. 1-9	32	xx. 3-4	101
xi. 10-32	33	xx. 24, 25	99
xi. 10—xiii. 18	40	xxi—xxiii	61
xii. 6-8	99	xxii—xxxii	55
xii. 24, 25	99	xxiii—xxiv	56
xiv. 3	14	xxv. 8	100
xiv. 1-7, 18-20	41	xxv. 10-22	101
xv. 1—xxi. 21	42	xxv. 17-22	31
xvii. 10-14	63	xxv—xl	100
xix. 37, 38	85	xxvii. 9-18	100
xxii. 1, 2, 14	100	xxix. 42-45	100
xxii—xxiv	43	xxxv—xl	55
xxv—xxvii	44	**LEVITICUS** i. 1-5	191
xxv. 7	33	i—xxii	56
xxviii. 10—xxxiv. 31	45	xiii. 8	132
xxviii. 18-22	99	xxv.	57
xxxv. 1-3, 6, 14, 15	99	xxvi. 11-12	101
xxxv. 1-20	46		
xxxv. 23-26	45	**NUMBERS** i—iv	57
xxxv. 28, 29	44	iii. 26-31	91
xxxvii—xl	46	iv. 5, 15, 19, 20	91
xli—xlv	47	vi—ix	57

	PAGES.		PAGES.
x. 11—xii. 16	57	xxiii—xxiv. 30	69
xiii—xiv.	38	xxiv. 2, 147	40
xvi	56	xxiv. 32	70
xvi—xviii.	58	**JUDGES** i.	70
xx—xxi. 3	58	ii. 6-10.	69
xxi. 4—xxiv. 25	59	ii—iii. 30.	72
xxv—xxvii. 11	60	iii. 31	73
xxxi—xxxii	60	iii. 19-26	63
xxxii. 1-38	67	v. 20.	65
xxxiv. 11	14	vi—ix.	74
xxxv.	60	vi. 27, 36	133
		x. 1-2	75
DEUTERONOMY i. 26	61	x. 3—xvi. 31.	76
iii. 17	14	xiv.	73
vii. 1-5	67	xvii—xviii.	70
xxi. 8-14	101	xix—xxi.	71
xiii. 6-9	115		
xvi. 16	101	**RUTH** i.	77
xxi. 23	65	ii—iv	78
xxvii—xxxiv	62	iv. 18-22	78
xxviii. 25, 52-68	145	**I SAMUEL** i. 9, 14-27	78
xxviii. 27	133	i. 9	100
		i—iv. 1	80
JOSHUA i—v.	63	ii. 12-17, 21-25	78
v. 7	14	ii. 27-36	78
vi—ix. 27	64	ii. 34	133
vii. 5	80	iii. 3	100
viii. 1	34	iii. 11-18.	79
x	55	iv. 1-18	79
xi—xii	66	v. 1—vii. 2	79
xii. 3	14	vii. 10	65
xiii	67	vii. 3-14	80
xiii. 27	14	vii. 12—viii 22	81
xiv	67	ix—xi.	84
xv—xix	68	ix. 1—xi. 13	81
xxi	67	x. 25.	83
xxii.	68	xi	85, 88
xxii. 10	27		

SCRIPTURE TEXTS.

	PAGES.		PAGES.
xii.	81	2 **SAMUEL** i. 18–27.	90
xiii.	88	i—ii. 4.	90
xiii. 8–15.	82	ii—vi	91
xiii—xiv. 46	84	vi. 1–12	100
xiv.	85	vii. 1–13	100
xiv. 47–48.	85, 88	vii—xi. 1.	92
xv.	85	xi—xiv.	93
xvi. 1–5.	88	xii. 26–31	92
xvi. 1–13	82	xv—xxi	94
xvi. 13.	79	xxi. 1–11	65
xvi. 14–23	86	xxi. 12–14	90
xvii. 12–58	89	xxi. 15–22	95
xvii—xviii. 5	85	xxiv	95
xviii. 6—xix. 10	86, 89	xxiv. 17–25	100
xix. 11–24.	86, 89	1 **KINGS** i. 1—ii. 11	95
xix. 13	88	iii. 1	97
xix. 16.	71	iii. 4—15, 16–28.	96
xix. 18–22	82	iv. 1–6	97
xix. 18–24	84, 88	iv. 7–28	98
xix. 20	117	iv. 11, 15.	97
xx. 18, 24–29.	88	iv. 22, 28	97, 98
xx—xxiv	86, 89	iv. 29–34	97
xxi. 1–9	88	iv. 34.	97
xxi. 7	85	v. 6, 8–12	98
xxii. 6–19	88	v. 7. 12.	97
xxii. 9, 18	85	v. viii.	100
xxii. 23	85	v. 13–18	97
xxv.	89	vi. 1, 38	100
xxv. 1	82	vi. 5–10	101
xxvi.	87, 89	vi. 7	98
xxvii.	89	vi. 16, 17	101
xxviii.	87, 89	vi. 31–33	101
xxviii. 3–25	83	vii. 13–45.	100
xxix.	89	vii. 15–22.	101
xxx.	89	vii. 27–39	101
xxxi	87, 88	vii. 48	101

	PAGES.		PAGES.
viii.	102	xvi. 1	108
viii. 8	97	xvi. 1-5, 7, 12	114
viii. 64	100	xvi. 16-29	108
ix. 11-14	48	xvi. 25	109
ix. 16, 24	97	xvi. 29—xvii. 1	109
ix. 20, 21	36	xvii.	115
ix. 23	97	xviii.	109, 115
ix. 26-28	98	xviii. 19, 22, 40	118
x. 1-8	97	xix.	115
x. 1-15	98	xix. 16-21	116
x. 22-25	98	xx.	110
x. 23, 24	97	xx. 13, 22	115
x. 28, 29	98	xx. 13-22	111
xi.	99	xx. 28, 35	111
xi. 1	97	xx. 34	109
xi. 9-13	103	xxi.	109
xi. 29	79, 105, 114	xxi. 17-29	115
xi. 29-39	103, 114	xxi. 19	110
xi. 30	105	xxii.	110, 112
xii. 1-19	103	xxii. 6—8, 22, 23	118
xii. 15	114	xxii. 8-28	115
xii. 20—xv. 8	104		
xii. 15, 22, 23	105	**2 KINGS** i. 1-18	110
xii. 22-24	114	i. 3—ii. 7	116
xii. 26-28	101	ii. 15-18	116
xiii. 1, 5-8	105	iii.	112
xiii. 1, 11	115	iii. 1-27	110
xiii. 2	138	iii. 2-19	116
xiii. 11	118	iii. 4	109
xiii. 11-31	105	iii. 8	115
xiv. 2-16	105	iv. 1-7	116
xiv. 2-18	114	iv. 42, 43	117
xiv. 21-31	97	v. 21-24	117
xv. 8—xvii. 20	106	vi. 1-10	116
xv. 24	112	vi. 12	116
xv. 25—xvi. 20	107	vi. 24—vii. 20	117
xv. 29	114	viii. 1-15	107

	PAGES.		PAGES.
viii. 16	113	xviii. 14—xix. 37	134
viii. 16-24	119	xx. 1-11	132
viii. 24-29	119	xx. 5-6	133
ix. 1-12	117	xx. 11	133
ix—xi	120	xx. 12-19	133
ix. 16-28	119	xx. 17	145
x. 30	124	xx. 17-18	149
xi. 2	121	xxi	135
xi. 12—xii. 16	121	xxi. 10-16	146
xi. 18	121	xxi. 19-26	136
xii. 4-15	102	xxii—xxiii. 30	137
xii. 17-21	121	xxii. 16-17	145
xiii. 1-9	121	xxiii. 16	138
xiii. 9—xiv. 1	122	xxiii. 24	71
xiii. 13	123	xxiii. 30—xxiv. 6	140
xiii. 14-21	117	xxiv. 1	149
xiii. 23	121	xxiv. 8-16	142
xiv. 1-22	123	xxiv. 10-16	149
xiv. 8-16	122	xxiv. 20	143
xiv. 16	123	xxv. 8-21	149
xiv. 23-29	124	xxv. 8-22	145
xiv. 25	123	xxv. 22-26	147
xv. 1	123	xxv. 27	150
xv. 1-7	124	xxv. 27-30,	142
xv. 5	126		
xv. 8-12	124	I CHRONICLES vi. 28-33	83
xv. 10-38	126	ix. 22	83
xvi. 1, 5	126	xi. 3	83
xvi. 1-20	127	xi—xvi,	91
xvi. 10-19	102	xvii—xx	92
xvii. 1-23	129	xx. 4-8	95
xvii. 6-41	130	xxi. 18-30	100
xvii. 13-20	127	xxii	95
xviii. 1	132	xxii. 1	100
xviii. 1-8	130	xxii. 14	100
xviii. 11	130	xxiii—xxvii	91
xviii. 14-16	132	xxvi	95

	PAGES.		PAGES.
xxvi. 28	83	xii. 9, 11	102
xxvii. 25-31	91	xii. 15	104, 105
xxviii. 11-19	100	xiii	104
xxviii. xxix.	95	xiii. 32	104, 114
xxix. 2-6	100	xiv—xvi.	106
xxix. 29	83	xv. 1-7	106, 108
		xv. 1-8	114
2 CHRONICLES i. 1-13	96	xvi. 1-10	107
i. 14	98	xvi. 7-10	108, 114
i. 16, 17	98	xvii.	112
ii. 2, 17, 18	97	xvii. 11	113
ii. 3-9	100	xviii.	110, 112
ii. 8-16	98	xviii. 7-27	115
iii. 1	100	xix. 1-3	112, 113
iii. 4, 5, 8, 10-13	101	xix. 2-3	114
iii—vii	100	xx. 2	113
iv. 1-9	101	xx. 5	100
vi. 11-16	100	xx. 14-17	113, 114
iv. 19	101	xx. 34	114
v. 1-6	102	xx. 37	112, 113. 114
v. 4-10	101	xxi. 1-20	119
vi. 1-2	101	xxi. 12-15	116
vii. 1-14	101	xxii. 1-9	119
viii. 4	98	xxii. 11	121
viii. 7, 8, 10, 11	97	xxiii. 10-13	136
viii. 17, 18	98	xxiii. 17	111
ix. 1-7	97	xxiii. 11-xxiv. 16	121
ix. 10, 11, 31, 14. 21, 22, 24.	98	xxiii. 21-25	136
		xxiv. 7	121
ix. 22, 23	97, 98	xxiv. 17-27	121
ix. 25, 26, 28	98	xxiv. 19	125
ix. 29	114	xxiv. 21	100
xi.	104	xxv.	123
xi. 2	105	xxv. 7, 15	115, 125
xi. 2-4	114	xxv. 17-24	122
xii. 2-9	104	xxvi.	124
xii. 5, 7, 15	114	xxvi. 5	125

	PAGES.		PAGES.
xxvi. 22, 23	135	xxii. 14	80
xxvii.	126	xxiii.	90
xxvii. 4–6	127	xxvii. 4	102
xxviii.	127	xxix.	90
xxix.	102	xxxiv.	90
xxx, xxxi	131	xl.	90
xxxii. 1–23	134	xliii. 1–4	102
xxxii. 31	133	xliv. 1–3	64
xxxiii. 1–18	102	xliv. 3	34
xxxiii.	135	xlvi. 1–5	100
xxxiv. 1–13	102	lii. 8	101
xxxiv. 29–33	102	liii.	80
xcxiv. 35	137	liv.	90
xxxv. 18	83	lvi.	90
xxvvi. 1–8	140	lvii.	90
xxxvi. 6, 7	149	lix.	80
xxxvi. 9, 10	142	lxiii.	90
xxxvi. 10	149	lxxviii. 60, 67	79
xxxvi. 11–21	104	lxxxiv.	101
xxxvi. 1–3	143	lxxxvii.	154
xxxvi. 16	143	xcii. 12–14	101
xxxvi. 17–31	145	xcvi. 1–13	91
xxxvi. 18–20	149	xcvii.	153
EZRA i—iii	153	xcvii. 5	65
iv—vi.	155	xcviii. 8	65
vii—x.	157	xcix.	153
NEHEMIAH i—xiii.	158	xcix. 6	79, 83
xii. 27 sq.	159	ciii.	90
ESTHER i—x.	156	ciii. 16	33
JOB ii. 7	133	cv. 1–15	91
xvi. 18	31	civ.	154
PSALMS vi.	90	cvi. 1, 47, 48	91
vii.	90	cvii.	154
viii.	90	cxiv.	63
xviii.	90	cxv.	153
xxi.	90	cxviii.	154
		cxxvi.	153

	PAGES.		PAGES.
cxxxii. 1–5	102	xxii. 11, 12	140
cxxxvii.	154	xxii. 18, 19	140
PROVERBS xxviii. 17	32	xxiii. 5, 6	142
		xxiv. 1	142
ISAIAH i. 1	125	xxiv.	145
x.	134	xxiv. 8, 9	148
xiii.	152	xxv.	140
xiv.	152	xxv. 8–38	145
xiv. 24–27	134	xxv. 11	149
xvii. 12	33	xxv. 12	152
xviii.	134	xxvi. 27	140
xix.	134	xxvii. 3	133
xx. 4–6	134	xxvii. 12–22	142
xxi. 9, 10	152	xxviii. 1–11	143
xxii. 1–14	134	xxviii. 4, 11	152
xxvi. 21	31	xxviii. 29	142
xxx. 1–7	134	xxix.	149, 150
xxxiv. 5	31	xxix. 1–20	143
xxxvi—xxxvii. 10	134	xxix. 17–21	148
xxxviii.	132	xxx.	148
xxxviii. 1–8	133	xxxii.	145
xxxviii. 17	133	xxxii—xxxiv.	142
xxxix.	133	xxxiv. 2, 3	145
xxxix. 2, 6	132	xxxv. 36	140
xl.	154	xxxvi. 2, 3	149
xli. 1–7	152	xxxvi. 10	101
xlvi. i.	79	xxxvii—xxxix.	142
xlviii. 20, 21	154	xxxix. 8–10	149
lv. 12	65	xl.	140
JEREMIAH i—x.	147, 139	xl. 1	148
iii. 18	150	xl—xliv.	147
vii. 12–14	79	xlii. 1–11	142
vii. 31, 32	136	xliv.	150
xiii. 18–21	142	xliv. 14, 27	148
xv. i	83	xlvi. 1–12	140
xxi. 1–10	142	xlvi. 10	31
xxi. 1—xxii. 9	145	xlvii.	140
xxii.	142	xlviii. 7	79

SCRIPTURE TEXTS.

	PAGES.		PAGES.
xlix. 3	79	iv. 15	63
l. 51	152	v. 1	124
li. 59-64	143	x. 6	79
lii. 12-23	102	**JOEL** i. 2	34
lii. 12-27	149	ii. 17	101
lii. 17-30	145	ii. 20	14
lii. 28-30	146, 149	**AMOS** i. 1	125
LAMENTATIONS ii. 19	80	ii. 7	124
EZEKIEL iii.	149	iii. 9, 12	124
viii.	150	iv. 1-8	124
ix. 3	31	v. 27	124
x. 18	31	vii. 17	124
xi. 14-25	149	**MICAH** iii. 12	145
xii. 21-28	149	iv. 10	109
xiii.	150	vi. 16	108
xiv.	149	vii. 13	145
xvii—xx.	149	**NAHUM** i—iii	137
xx. 20-22	149	**ZEPHANIAH** i. 2-6	145
xxvii. 7-15	36	i—iii	137
xxviii. 14	31	ii. 12	31
xxxiii. 34	149	**ZECHARIAH** vii.	150
xxxvi.	147	x. 2	71
xxxviii. 2-6	36		
xl. 45, 46	101		
xl—xlvi	100	NEW TESTAMENT.	
xlii. 1-6	101	**MATTHEW** i. 5	64
xlvii. 18	14	xii. 38	133
DANIEL i.	149	xvi. 1	133
i. 16-21	151	**MARK** xxviii. 5	94
i. 19-21	150	**LUKE** i. 45-55, 67-79	80
ii.	149, 151	ii. 36	80
ii. 46-49	150	iv. 25	115
xi. 8	79	**ACTS** ii. 5	34
HOSEA i. 1	125		
iii. 4	71		
iv. 13	124		

	PAGES.		PAGES.
ROMANS i. 8	34	**JAMES** ii. 5	64
iii. 25	56	v. 17	115
1 COR. i. 30	56		
2 COR. xi. 3	30	**2 PETER** ii. 5	34
HEBREWS vii. 1–11	41	**REVELATIONS** xii. 9	35
ix. 22	101	xx. 2	30
xi. 31	64		

REFERENCE BOOKS
FOR
BIBLE STUDENTS.

JAMIESON, FAUSSET & BROWN'S Popular Portable Commentary. Critical, Practical, Explanatory. Four volumns in neat box, fine cloth, $8.00; half bound, $10.00.

    A new edition, containing the complete unabridged notes in clear type on good paper, in four handsome 12 mo. volumes of about 1.000 pages each, with copious index, numerous illustrations and maps, and a Bible Dictionary compiled from Dr. Wm. Smith's standard work.
    Bishop Vincent of Chautauqua fame says: "The *best* condensed commentary on the whole Bible is Jamieson, Fausset & Brown."

CRUDEN'S UNABRIDGED CONCORDANCE TO THE HOLY SCRIPTURES. With life of the author. 864 pp., 8vo., cloth (net), $1.00; half roan, sprinkled edges (net), 2.00; half roan, full gilt edges (net), $2.50.

SMITH'S BIBLE DICTIONARY, comprising its Antiquities, Biography, Geography and Natural History, with numerous maps and illustrations. Edited and condensed from his great work by WILLIAM SMITH, LL. D. 776 pages. 8vo, many illustrations, cloth, $1.50.

THE BIBLE TEXT CYCLOPEDIA. A complete classification of Scripture Texts in the form of an alphabetical list of subjects. By Rev. JAMES INGLIS. Large 8vo, 524 pages, cloth, $1.75.

    The plan is much the same as the "Bible Text Book" with the valuable additional help in that the texts referred to are quoted in full. Thus the student is saved the time and labor of turning to numerous passages, which, when found, may not be pertinent to the subject he has in hand.

THE TREASURY OF SCRIPTURE KNOWLEDGE; consisting of 500,000 scripture references and parallel passages, with numerous notes. 8vo, 778 pages. cloth, $2.00.

    A single examination of this remarkable compilation of references will convince the reader of the fact that "the Bible is its own best interpreter."

THE WORKS OF FLAVIUS JOSEPHUS, translated by WILLIAM WHISTON, A. M., with Life, Portrait, Notes and Index. A new cheap edition in clear type. Large 8vo, 684 pages, cloth, $2.00.

100,000 SYNONYMS AND ANTONYMS. By Rt. Rev. SAMUEL FALLOWS, A. M., D. D. 512 pages, cloth, $1.00.

    A complete Dictionary of synonyms *and words of opposite* meanings, with an appendix of Briticisms, Americanisms, Colloquialisms, Homonims, Homophonous words, Foreign Phrases, etc., etc.
    "This is one of the best books of its kind we have seen, and probably there is nothing published in the country that is equal to it."—*Y. M. C. A. Watchman.*

NEW YORK: **Fleming H. Revell**   CHICAGO:
12 Bible House, Astor Pl.   148 & 150 Madison St

By-Paths of Bible Knowledge.

"The volumes issuing under the above general title fully deserve success. They have been entrusted to scholars who have a special acquaintance with the subjects about which they severally treat."—*Athenæum.*

> These books are written by specialists, and their aim is to give the results of the latest and best scholarships on questions of Biblical history, science and archæology. The volumes contain much information that is not easily accessible, even to those who have a large acquaintance with the higher literature on these subjects.

15. **Early Bible Songs.**
    With introduction on the Nature and Spirit of Hebrew Song, by A. H. Drysdale M. A. $1 00
14. **Modern Discoveries on the Site of Ancient Ephesus.**
    By J. T. Wood, F. S. A. Illustrated. $1 00
13. **The Times of Isaiah.**
    As illustrated from Contemporary Monuments. By A. H. Sayce, LL. D. .80
12. **The Hittites; or the Story of a Forgotten Empire.**
    By A. H. Sayce, LL. D. Illustrated. Crown, 8vo. $1 20
11. **Animals of the Bible.**
    By H. Chichester Hart, Naturalist to Sir G. Nares' Arctic Expedition and Professor Hull's Palestine Expedition. Illustrated, Crown, 8vo $1 20
10. **The Trees and Plants Mentioned in the Bible.**
    By W. H. Groser, B. Sc. Illustrated $1 00
9. **The Diseases of the Bible.**
   By Sir J. Risdon Bennett $1 00
8. **The Dwellers on the Nile.**
   Chapters on the Life, Literature, History and Customs of Ancient Egypt. By E. A. Wallis Budge, M. A., Assistant in Department of Oriental Antiquities, British Museum. Illustrated $1 20
7. **Assyria; Its Princes, Priests and People.**
   By A. H. Sayce, M. A., LL. D., author of "Fresh Light from Ancient Monuments," "Introduction to Ezra, Nehemiah and Esther," etc. Illustrated $1 20
6. **Egypt and Syria.**
   Their Physical Features in Relation to Bible History. By Sir J. W. Dawson, Principal of McGill College, Montreal, F. G. S., F. R. S., author of "The Chain of Life in Geological Time." etc. Second edition, revised and enlarged. With many illustrations $1 20
5. **Galilee in the time of Christ.**
   By Selah Merrill, D. D., author of "East of the Jordan," etc. With Map $1 00
4. **Babylonian Life and History.**
   By E. A. Willis Budge, M. A., Cambridge, Assistant in the Department of Oriental Antiquities, British Museum, illustrated $1 20
3. **Recent Discoveries on the Temple Hill at Jerusalem.**
   By the Rev. J. King, M. A., Authorized Lecturer for the Palestine Exploration Fund. With Maps, Plans and Illustrations $1 00
2. **Fresh Lights From the Ancient Monuments.**
   A Sketch of the most striking Confirmations of the Bible from recent discoveries in Egypt, Assyria, Babylonia, Palestine and Asia Minor. By A. H. Sayce, LL. D., Deputy Professor of Comparative Philology, Oxford, etc. With fac-similes from photographs $1 20
1. **Cleopatra's Needle.**
   History of the London Obelisk, with an Exposition of the Hieroglyphics. By the Rev. J. King, Lecturer for the Palestine Exploration Fund. With Illustrations $1 00

NEW YORK, **Fleming H. Revell Co.** CHICAGO,
12 Bible House, Astor Pl.   148 & 150 Madison St.

www.ingramcontent.com/pod-product-compliance
Lightning Source LLC
Chambersburg PA
CBHW030401230426
43664CB00007BB/687